The Chalet Host's Bible

If you're dreaming of doing a season as a ski chalet host then this book is for you!

It's the definitive indispensable guide to all you need to know about chalet hosting.

It assumes you can already cook beans on toast and know a saucepan when you see one, but everything else is explained.

It's crammed full of tested recipes, of course, but that's just the start. It covers breakfast, afternoon tea, dinner, wine, cheese, kids' food, vegetarians, special diets, Xmas, presentation – everything.

There's a pile of advice and tips-of-the-trade about managing the chalet including cleaning, budgeting, shopping, storage, log fires, saunas etc.

It even covers guest relations – dealing with 'The Good, The Bad, and The Ugly'!

Minimum effort, maximum impact – maximum skiing.

Written in an easy chatty style by chalet hosts with over 10 years of experience. We've also run a cookery school so we know a thing or two about cooking, and about teaching.

The only thing better than this Bible is actually being there... working as a chalet host.

Coco Cookery

Coco Cookery runs cookery courses specifically aimed at people wanting to run a ski chalet. It is owned and operated by Anne and Jeff Pratt who have run ski chalets for over ten seasons.

Students on our courses receive hands-on cooking tuition and tons of advice. The following publications are given to all students and are now published and available to non-students too.

The Chalet Host's Bible

The Coco Cookery Guide To Getting A Ski Job

Together these books will help make your dream come true.

Anne & Jeff welcome comments at their website
www.CocoCookery.co.uk

Students' comments on Coco Cookery

"... I didn't realise how easy it is to follow a recipe - IF YOU READ IT !!"
Georgie, got a job with GoSkiMeribel.

"... delivers everything as stated on the tin!"
Rob, now has to convince his wife to do a season!

"... wicked food... keeps it all simple..."
Cara, ready for those job interviews.

"... feel ready to run my own chalet..."
Georgia, secured job with SkiVal in St Anton.

"... now feel VERY confident as a chalet host..."
Amelia & Joss, it's difficult for an 18 year old couple to get a job together but they impressed SkiBeat.

"... the Bible is brilliant..."
Lewis, secured job with SkiBeat.

"... gold mines of all things ski hosting."
Jonathan & Amy, secured job with SkiVal.

The Chalet Host's Bible

**by Anne and Jeff Pratt
of Coco Cookery**

Get a life - not just a job

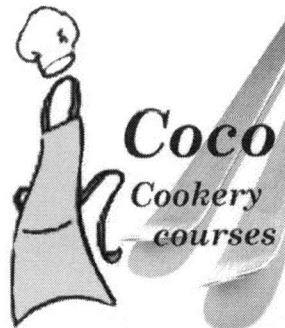

www.CocoCookery.co.uk

You can find photos & videos of many of the recipes in this book at
www.cococookery.co.uk/foodpics/

Published by Mallaktech (www.mallaktech.co.uk)
First created for Coco Cookery students in 2010
First published as an ebook in 2016
Published in paperback in 2017

Contents

Introduction 1

Hygiene & Safety 5

Menus 7
   Menu planning 7
   Menu timing 11

Terminology & Techniques 15
   Basic 15
   Cooking at altitude 17
   Knives & chopping 17
   Pots, pans & dishes 18
   The oven 18
   Cook thoroughly 19
   Frying & sweating 19
   Oils, butter & grease 19
   Measuring 20
   Scaling 21
   Seasoning, herbs & spices 21
   Rice 22
   Pasta 22
   Thickening sauces 23
   Roux sauce 23
   Chocolate 23
   Eggs 23
   Cream 23
   Onions 24
   Cheese 24
   Flour 24
   Pastry 24
   Preparing to cook 25
   While you're cooking 26
   After cooking 26

Recipes 27

   Breakfasts 28
      Porridge 29
      Croissants 29
      Scrambled Eggs 30
      Boiled Eggs 30
      Fried Eggs 30
      Poached Eggs 30
      Ouefs En Pain 30
      French Toast 30
      Bacon & Sausages 31
      Tomatoes, Beans & Mushrooms 31
      Apple Rings 31
      Pancakes (Crepes) 32
      American Pancakes 33

Cakes..34
   Yoghurt Cakes...35
      Simple sponge cake..35
      Lemon drizzle cake...35
      Date and walnut loaf...35
      Chocolate cake..36
      Coffee and walnut smiley cake..36
      Marmalade cake..36
      Apple and cinnamon cake...36
      Coconut ski cake...36
      Carrot and ginger cake...36
   Country Fruit Loaf (All Bran Cake)..37
   Fruit & Nut Bars...37
   Chocolate Krispie Cakes...37
   Banana Chocolate Brownies..38
   Flapjacks...38
   Coconut Macaroons..39
   Flourless Chocolate Brownies...39
   Ginger Snaps..39
   Banana Bread...40
   Moist Carrot and Ginger Cake...40
   Diabetic Fruit Cake...41
   Shortbread...41

Aperitifs...42
   Kir Royale...42
   Canaletto (Raspberry fizz)...42
   Champagne Cocktail..42
   Buck's Fizz..42
   Mock Bellini..42
   Calimocho...42
   Vin Chaud...43
   Mulled White Wine...43

Canapes...44
   Cucumber Cups With Smoked Salmon Tartare....................................44
   Smoked Salmon Blinis..44
   Honey & Mustard Glazed Sausages..44
   Cream Cheese And Pepper Wraps..45
   Cheese And Olive Scones..45
   Blue Cheese And Walnut Crostini...45
   Goats Cheese Crostinis...45
   Pissaladiere..46
   Spicy Smashed Chickpeas..46
   Marinated Olives...46
   Pesto Whirls...46
   Cheese Straws...47
   Devils And Angels...47
   Stuffed Mushrooms...47
   Cheese Discs..47
   Frogs' Legs..47
   Snails In Garlic Butter..48

Tomato Bruschettas..48

Sauces & Dressings..49
Vinaigrette Salad Dressing...49
Balsamic Vinegar Dressing..49
Balsamic Jus..49
Sweet Chilli Sauce..49
Marie Rose Sauce..49
Mustard Mayonnaise Dressing..50

Starters 51
Salad Savoyarde..51
Chickpea And Ginger Salad...51
Roasted Tomato, Mozzarella and Pesto Salad 51
Rocket, Pear And Parmesan Salad 52
Prawn Cocktail 52
Salmon Mousse...52
Apple & Reblochon (or Brie) Bruschetta..52
Margherita Salad...53
Crispy Duck Salad With Spicy Plum Sauce...53
Caramelised Red Onion Tarts..54
Penne Alle Salmone..54
Cheese Risotto (and Mushroom Risotto)..55
Thai Fishcakes With Sweet Chilli Sauce..55
Baked Camembert With Crusty Bread 56
Cheese Fondue..56
Artichoke Heart & Parmesan Gratins 57
Seafood Gratins...57
Fish Finger Gratins...57
Soupe du Jour..58
Soupe du Savoyarde..58
French Onion Soup..58
Leek and Potato Soup 59
Tuscan Bean Soup 59
Quick Tomato Soup..60
Red Lentil Soup..60
Carrot And Coriander Soup...60

Main Courses 61
Chicken Recipes...61
Chicken in Cheese and Cider Sauce..61
Coq Au Vin...61
Chicken Basque...62
Slow-roasted Chicken...62
Hunter's Chicken (Chicken Chasseur)...63
Chicken Provencal 63
Chicken Montagnarde...64
Thai Curry (Red or Green) 64
Moroccan Chicken..65
Turkey recipes..66
Turkey Stroganoff...66
Creamy Lemon Turkey Fricassée...66
Turkey and Mushroom Pie...67

Pork Recipes...68
    Pork Stuffed With Apricots (or Prunes), Cooked In Cider.............68
    Normandy Pork Chops..68
    Roast Pork...69
Lamb Recipes...70
    Roast Lamb...70
    Lamb & Apricot Tagine..71
    Lamb Shanks..71
Beef Recipes...72
    Lasagne (With Coleslaw & Garlic Bread).................................72
    Boeuf Bourguignonne..74
Duck Recipes...75
    Confit De Canard...75
Salmon Recipes...76
    Salmon With Pesto And Parmesan...76
    Salmon En Croute...76
    Oven Baked Salmon With Chilli And Ginger...............................76
Savoyarde Specialities...77
    Savoyarde Chicken..77
    Tartiflette..78

Vegetables 79
    Olive Oil & Sea Salt Baked Potatoes (Hasselback) 79
    Roasted Sweet Potato Chips 79
    Gratin Dauphinois..80
    Potatoes Boulangere..80
    Mustard Mash...80
    Lyonnaise Potatoes...81
    Sweet Potato Rostis..81
    Pan Fried Leeks..81
    Couscous With Roasted Mediterranean Vegetables.........................82
    Vegetable Pilau Rice...82
    Orange Braised Red Cabbage...83
    Savoury Spring Cabbage...83
    'Vichy' Carrots..83
    Oven Roasted Root Vegetables...84
    Wilted Spinach...84

Desserts 85
    Lemon Posset...85
    Banana Bakewell..85
    Caramelised Apples 85
    Baked Bananas..86
    Black Forest Pavlova...86
    Tarte Tatin..87
    Citrus Apple Flan with Syllabub..87
    Jaffa Pudding..88
    White Chocolate Cheesecake With Raspberry Coulis.......................88
    Lemon & Lime Cheesecake..89
    Lemon Tart...89
    Banana Brioche and Butter Pudding......................................90
    Apricot Crumble 90

Mango (or Apricot) Fool 90
Sticky Toffee Pudding with Orange Toffee Sauce 91
Petit Pots Au Chocolat...91
Forest Fruit Crisp...92
Tiramisu...92
Chocolate Mousse..92
Quick Chocolate Sauce 93
Butterscotch Sauce...93
Galets aux Fruits Confit..93

Special dietary requirements 94
Vegetarian 97
Chick Pea Tagine 97
Mushroom Ragout..97
Stuffed Pepper 98
Melanzane 98
Roasted Peppers With Beans And Goats' Cheese........................99
Lentil Roast 99
Asparagus and Red Pepper Filo Parcels 99
Surprise De Legumes 100
Chilli Beans 100
Cream Cheese & Roasted Red Pepper Parcels 101
Chick Pea Patties With Raita 101
Hazelnut Roast 102
Vegetable Tart Tatin 102

Kids 103
Fish Pie 103
Chicken Goujons 103
Beef Burgers 103
Nikki's Mash Mountains 104
Potato Wedges..104
Sweet And Sour Chicken 104
Spaghetti Carbonara 104
Pizza 105
Cottage Pie 105
Spaghetti Bolognaise 105
Macaroni Cheese..106
Pork Schnitzel..106
Pasta With Pesto And Parmesan...106
Spaghetti With Marmite 106
Spaghetti With Spicy Sardines 106
Kids Desserts..107

Cheeseboard...108

Wine...110

Christmas cooking made easy..111

Presentation...118
Garnishing 118
Table laying..120

Afternoon tea...121
Napkin folding...121

Money Matters 124

Cleaning...128

Guests..132

Miscellaneous 136
Leftovers..136
Coping with disasters..136
Fires...137
Honesty Bars...138
Saunas and Jacuzzis..138

And finally… making the most of it 140

Check lists..147
Things to take with you...147
Driving to resort..148
Leaving your house empty...148

French Translations 149

INTRODUCTION

Would you like to spend five months in the mountains?
How about skiing or snowboarding almost every day?
Swapping the miserable British winter for sun and snow?

Then why not be a chalet host for a season? You don't need to be a cordon bleu cook, or have any previous ski-related experience to be a chalet host; nor do you have to be on a graduate gap year! All sorts of people become chalet hosts. The key skills required are enthusiasm, organisation and an empathy with (or at least, a *tolerance* of!) your guests.

A winter season is an unforgettable experience. Yes, of course it is hard work, but the payback is great. You will gain valuable organisational and culinary skills while having the time of your life. It will count as a plus on your CV for almost any future job.

We are about to return for yet another season as (mature) chalet hosts in the French Alps, having done our long stint in the rat race while raising a family. We owe it all to our daughter, Ruth, who firstly introduced us to the joys of skiing, and then sowed the seeds of a hankering for a mid-life gap year! One year was simply not enough; we are hooked and over 10 years later, it has become a great lifestyle.

We don't want to upset those who have crossed to the dark side (i.e. boarders), but we are skiers and so for the rest of this book, please take 'ski' to mean 'ski or board'.

We believe that this book will tell you all you need to know about doing a successful winter season; it contains lots of easy tried and tested recipes, plus tips on running the chalet and making the most of your time. It was originally written to accompany our chalet cookery course and serve as a reference book for our students, and we have now augmented it and made it available to those hankering for a chalet host job but who may not need a chalet cooking course.

WARNING: ONE SEASON MAY NOT BE ENOUGH

How this book is arranged

We assume that you know a little about what a chalet host is, and a little about the ski scene in general, otherwise why would you be reading this book? So we don't go into lots of detail about things you probably already know. We concentrate on the ski chalet culture in France because that's where the vast majority of chalets are found, and where we have amassed our experience.

This book is not designed to be read end-to-end; dip into it as you need, whether it's for an exciting recipe, or how to clean the toilet.

The first part of the book covers basic cooking stuff: hygiene, menus, terms, techniques and ingredients. Some of this you may know already but it's worth repeating and we emphasise where this may differ from your normal home cooking.

We assume you will have read this section before using any of our recipes!!

Next comes a whole heap of recipes – everything from a simple sauce to a full blown roast dinner. Starters, main courses, desserts – they're all covered. There's even special sections for kids' food and special diets. All our recipes have been tried and tested in a ski resort.

Then comes the chalet management stuff – cleaning, budgeting, shopping, and of course how to handle guests. We show you how to get organised and save lots of time, time better spent skiing.

Finally, we tell you what to expect, what to take, and how to maximise your enjoyment in the snow.

What is a chalet host?

In Europe, many people taking ski holidays prefer to stay in a chalet rather than a hotel. A chalet is rather like an ordinary home that has new guests to stay every week. The menu and meal times are generally fixed but it is less formal than a hotel and a lot less impersonal. A chalet host is responsible for the day to day running of a ski chalet. She (or he – yes, lots of guys run chalets too!) runs the chalet as if it was her home. She cooks all the meals, goes shopping, cleans the chalet and generally looks after the guests for 6 days a week (having one day off each week), whilst the guests ski all day long! In addition to cooking and cleaning, she has to be sociable and informative. While you are not expected to entertain the guests by telling jokes and dancing on the table, you do need to show an interest and talk to them.

Most companies appoint a single chalet host for small chalets (up to about 8 guests), and a pair of hosts for medium chalets (9-16) people; often these chalets are run by couples or friends who have applied together.

Some companies have larger chalets (sometimes called chalet hotels) which operate on a slightly different system; there is a chef (and possibly a sous chef) doing all the cooking, and often a washer-up. In this set up chalet hosts do not need to be able to cook; they clean, lay tables and serve meals but may be required to prepare vegetables or other kitchen tasks.

Smaller chalets tend to be booked by one party of guests, whereas the larger ones often have several groups who do not know each other.

Chalets vary tremendously in their quality and hence their target marketplace; from basic no frills up to high end luxury. Their hosts must also reflect the standards of the company.

All the ski companies that we know of require applicants to be over 18 and many prefer chalet hosts to be over 21, and they positively welcome "mature" applicants (even active pensioners), as well as the traditional gap year students. Many British companies only employ UK citizens and others will consider you providing you have a

UK bank account and a UK National Insurance number. You are unlikely to get a post in the USA without having done a season in Europe first.

A Day in the Life of a Chalet Host

The timetable below is a guide to what to expect for a typical day as a chalet host, once you are organised. To start with you may feel that virtually all your waking life is spent working. Don't despair! It will get better as you get into the swing of things. If it doesn't, you are doing something wrong so ask for help and guidance. You are not there solely to work; if you don't get your snow time you will be a very grumpy host, which won't make a good impression on the guests. In addition, you will not last the season if you are unhappy, and that is not good for the company.

Some days may be longer if your guests are late or tarry over dinner; on other days your guests might have finished breakfast by 8.30 and you will be able to hit the slopes before 10am.

7.00am	wake up, shower and get to work.
7.20am	prepare porridge, make tea/coffee for yourself.
	clear up any mess from previous night.
	lay table and set out cereals, juices etc.
	prepare items for cooked breakfast.
	eat cereal/fruit/yoghurt to give yourself some energy.
8.00am	guests appear, cook breakfast to order.
9.00am	make a cake.
9.30am	breakfast finished.
	clear table, wash up.
	check ingredients for dinner.
	prep for dinner.
	sit down, coffee and croissant.
10.00am	clean rooms.
	lay up afternoon tea.
11.00am	Ski Time!!
5.00pm	prepare children's teas.
	(possibly prepare your own dinner).
	clear away afternoon tea.
6.00pm	start cooking dinner.
	serve children's teas.
	eat own dinner.
	get wines ready for dinner.
6.30pm	make canapés.
	lay table.
	cook dinner.
7.30pm	serve canapés and aperitifs.
8.00pm	serve dinner, including coffee.
9.30pm	clear table, wash up.
	empty rubbish.
	check food needed for tomorrow's menu.
10.30pm	Free Time - party, socialise, sleep etc
	BUT make sure you get up for breakfast!!

No one said it would be easy!

But with the help of this book and a bit of organisation (actually, a lot of organisation), you'll sail through the workload and hit the slopes on most days. It's why you're there.

First, some essentials before you start cooking.

HYGIENE & SAFETY

Food hygiene is of the utmost importance, and will almost certainly be covered in pre-season training by your company, or they may insist you obtain training before you go. Your responsibility to your guests and the company cannot be overstated. Here are the key elements to consider but **do not** assume this replaces the need for further study.

Wash your hands

The most important thing to remember is to wash your hands often, using hot water and antibacterial hand cleaner. Always wash hands after touching: high-risk foods such as raw meat and eggs, rubbish, your hair and especially after using the loo. Keep a separate towel for drying hands, rather than using the tea towel.

Keep towels and cloths clean

Although there are plenty of disposable washing up cloths available, it is cheaper and more environmentally friendly to buy washable cloths. You must wash them regularly and at high temperatures to kill off any bugs and bacteria. Cloths, sponges, brushes and scourers can be washed in the dishwasher on a hot cycle with the pots and pans.
Remember to keep different cloths for different cleaning jobs – you can't just use one cloth for the floor, worktops and washing up, however often you wash them. We use *'pink for sinks, blue for loos'*.
It is also important to change your tea towels regularly and wash on a hot cycle. Don't let guests use your towels if possible; they'll try and dry their hands on your tea towels!

Keep the kitchen clean

Keep your kitchen spotlessly clean, particularly fridge and freezer, sinks, dustbins and work surfaces. Wipe everything down regularly with antibacterial kitchen spray. Empty bins at least once a day. Clean the fridge at least once-a-week – just before shopping day is best when it's empty.

Personal hygiene

Remove jewellery, wear a clean apron and roll up your sleeves before you start preparing food. If your hair is long, tie it back before you start cooking and try not to touch your hair or face while you are working. Some companies insist you wear a hat in the kitchen – no, not a beanie!
Always take off your apron before going to the loo and wash your hands thoroughly afterwards.
Wash utensils immediately after testing/tasting food and don't use your fingers to dip into sauces to test them.

Avoid cross contamination

Raw meat and eggs can contain bacteria which are easily transferred to your hands, cooking equipment such as spoons, pans or chopping boards. These bacteria are destroyed by heat, which is why all meat and eggs should be thoroughly cooked before serving. In particular, pork and chicken should never be served with even a hint of pink.
You should prepare raw meat separately from cooked meat and all other food stuffs. Keep a separate chopping board for raw meat and scrub it regularly with hot water and detergent or wash in a hot cycle of the dishwasher. Ideally use coloured boards: red for meat, blue for fish, green for veg, white for dairy; or mark the boards with permanent ink.
The same goes for utensils: wash knives etc immediately after cutting meat and fish.
Store raw meat and fish on the bottom shelf of your fridge, and food that is ready to be eaten on the shelves above. This means that raw foods can't drip on to cooked foods and cross contaminate them. Use boxes or trays to prevent drips and spillages.

Store food correctly

Check sell-by dates regularly, take care to use the oldest first and throw out any mouldy or out of date food. Keep in mind the old saying, *'If in doubt, throw it out'*.
Make sure your fridge and freezer are kept at the correct temperatures; do not leave the fridge door open any longer than necessary. Fridges must be kept below 8C (ideally between 2 and 5C); freezers below -18C; in some

chalets (definitely in Austria) you'll have to keep a daily log of temperatures. Try to keep guests out of your fridge; use an honesty bar fridge for tea-time milk and butter if possible.

All food should be covered, either in its original package/jar or by using clingfilm or foil. Anything not in its packaging should be labelled to identify its contents and it's good practice to state the use-by date (mandatory in Austria!).

Raw meats should be at the bottom of the fridge with cooked meats and salads above them, and dairy above those.

Freezing food

Companies vary in their attitudes to freezing food that you have prepared, so you will need to adhere to their guidelines. Some follow French Law to the letter and prohibit any freezing of chalet cooked food. Others permit freezing food for staff use and some turn a blind eye!

Always defrost frozen food, including vegetables, thoroughly before cooking.

If you are permitted to freeze food, make sure that you do so as soon as possible after cooking (once the food is cool!) and defrost/reheat thoroughly before serving. It's good practice to note when the food was bought, when cooked and when frozen – this is mandatory in Austria.

Safe practices

- ➢ Don't leave metal spoons in hot pans
- ➢ Don't leave knives & glasses in the washing up bowl
- ➢ Don't leave pan handles over a gas flame
- ➢ Always carry sharp knives with the point downwards and the sharp edge to the rear
- ➢ Don't attempt to catch a falling knife
- ➢ Always cut/chop on a board, never in your hand
- ➢ Only reheat food once
- ➢ Always clear any spillages immediately
- ➢ Don't use a damp cloth for carrying hot pans/dishes
- ➢ Don't wear sandals, open shoes, (or barefoot) in the kitchen
- ➢ Use a fire blanket not an extinguisher on fat fires
- ➢ Tie back long hair
- ➢ Remove jewellery
- ➢ Keep work surfaces as clear as possible

Checkout the internet for full hygiene & safety regulations. In particular, the FSA (Food Standards Agency) has comprehensive details and various self-study media.

MENUS

MENU PLANNING

Some ski companies provide detailed menu plans to which you must adhere rigidly. Others have a suggested menu from which you are allowed to deviate once you have proved your ability. Some simply set a budget and leave you to get on with it!

Devising a menu plan is not as easy as it first appears. The meals must be nutritionally and visually balanced; they must come within budget; you must be able to cook the entire meal within the constraints of your kitchen. Most chalet kitchens are fairly basic: they have usually been designed for a French holiday home. For example, you will probably only have a single domestic oven/grill so you will not have space to cook a cheese soufflé starter, followed by a full roast dinner and then a hot apple pie! Also, you will not be able to cook dishes requiring different oven temperatures at the same time.

You also need to consider the pots, pans, dishes, crockery etc that you will need, both for cooking and serving the meal. For example, you probably won't have enough ramekins to use for both starter and dessert; if you need bowls for both starter and dessert, you may have to wash them out between courses.

An added complication comes courtesy of special dietary requirements (the bane of a chalet host's life!). That one vegetarian option can be the straw that breaks the camel's back as far as oven space goes.

Your menus will be restricted by the availability of food as well as budgets. Again, ski companies vary in their approach to shopping. Some will take you to the nearest supermarket and let you pick your own food, some have a strict lists of items which you may buy; some will actually import specialist foodstuffs from UK (e.g. bacon, mincemeat, marmalade, sausages). Generally, you will shop only once a week so fresh foods like salads need to be served soon after shopping day.

Most ski companies will expect you to prepare a full 3 course dinner each night, and in addition many also offer canapés, cheeseboard and coffee.

The main criterion is that your guests must enjoy the meals, which should be varied, well presented and taste good. You should be proud of the meals you serve, and they must be served on time. Your guests will be paying a lot of money to sample your cooking, so you owe it to them, and your company, to give them a superb culinary experience! Try to make each evening meal like a dinner party that you would prepare for friends. The meals should be rather more special than your normal weekday fare at home. The recipes given later are all fairly easy and foolproof (there's a challenge!).

The main meat/fish courses during the week will probably be chicken, lamb, pork, duck, salmon and beef, so you need at least one recipe for each of these.

When planning a menu, it is a good idea to have at least one course that can be prepared in advance, to ease the pressure in the evening. You will often find that guests are keen to chat about their day when you arrive to start cooking in the evening, especially if your kitchen is open plan. You need to be charming and attentive while you really just want to get on with the preparation.

It is worth spending time at the beginning of your season, getting a menu that works for you. You can then use it every week, and will find that it saves you a lot of time both shopping and cooking. It may sound boring, but it is new to each set of guests! Occasionally you may get guests staying for more than a week, so you will need to have a few alternative recipes.

Aim for a balanced, varied, interesting, attractive meal at each dinner, e.g. not salad for both starter and main course, nor pastry for main and dessert, nor beige looking meat, potato and vegetables, nor potato mash every day. As far as possible, adapt the starter and main course for vegetarians so that you do not cook completely different meals.

On changeover day when guests are coming and going, ensure that the food can cope with delayed flights and transfers.

Be flexible with your menus; if you find that something is not working, change it.

Sample 6 day menu plan

	Sat	Sun	Mon	Tues	Thurs	Fri
Afternoon cake	Chocolate krispies	All bran loaf	Chocolate banana brownies	Lemon drizzle, Apple & cinnamon cakes	Flapjacks	Coffee and walnut cake
Aperitif	Calimocho	Kir Royale	Raspberry fizz	Bellini	Buck's fizz	Vin chaud
Canapés	Pesto whirls & Cucumber cups	Tomato, cheese and olive skewers & Pate on toast	Stuffed mushrooms & Garlic snails	Smoked salmon blinis. & Stuffed vine leaves	Goats cheese wraps & Devils and angels	Cheese straws Honey roasted sausages
Starter	Salad savoyarde (Veg: omit lardons)	Caramelised red onion tarts	Apple and reblochon bruschettas	French onion soup	Prawn bake (Veg: mushroom bake)	Saucisson platter (Veg:cheese)
Meat/fish	Lamb tagine	Slow cooked chicken with sweet chilli sauce	Pork roti stuffed with apricots and poached in cider	Chicken breast stuffed with boursin and baked in wine	Confit du canard with red wine jus	Salmon en croute
Vegetarian	Chick pea tagine	Chilli beans	Chick pea patties	Vegetable and mozzarella tian	Mushroom ragout	Asparagus en croute
Potato/rice/ pasta	Couscous	Pilau rice with peas, peppers and sweetcorn	Mustard mash	Jacket potatoes	Dauphinoise potatoes	Hasselback potatoes
Vegetables	Roasted Mediterranean vegetables		Pan fried leeks	Vichy carrots	Green beans and minted peas	Salad
Dessert	Lemon posset	Tarte aux fines pommes	Banana brioche and butter pudding	White choc cheesecake with raspberry coulis	Chocolate pavlova	Petit pots au chocolat
Kids	Spaghetti carbonara & lemon posset	sweet & sour chicken, rice & fruit kebabs with choc sauce	pork schnitzel, mash, green beans & banana splits	chicken goujons, carrots , mash mountains & yoghurts	burgers, b/beans, potato wedges & meringues & ice cream	Fish pie, peas & choc pots

In the sample menu above:
- Saturday is changeover day
- there are two cakes to be made on Tuesday, as Wednesday is the host's day off
- Friday is shopping day (so the salad is fresh)
- Breakfast has been omitted as it's usually straightforward

Sample chalet plan

Once you've established your menu then it's a good idea to add to it the various other ad-hoc tasks that you must do during the week, e.g.

	Sat	Sun	Mon	Tues	Thur	Fri
Morning tasks	*Cook croissants for leavers.*		*Order meat.*		*Defrost prawns, beans & peas.*	*Clean fridge/freezers.*
Afternoon cake						
Afternoon tasks			*Company team meeting.*			*Check van/clear snow etc for tomorrow's leavers.*
Aperitif						
Canapés						
Starter						
Meat/fish						
Potato/rice/pasta						
Vegetables						
Dessert						
Evening tasks	*Defrost chicken breasts*			*Tell guests about day-off; check stocks.*	*Make shopping list.*	*Defrost croissants*

N.B.
  ➢ Some menu items have been omitted for clarity.
  ➢ You could add regular tasks too, e.g. put breakfast juices in the fridge each evening.

MENU TIMING

At the start of the season, it is a good idea to work out a timetable for preparing dinner for each day, in order to make sure that everything is ready at the right time. You don't want to start work too early and be hanging around but you don't want to start too late and find dinner is late. If you put all the thinking *once* into planning the timetable then you won't need to think much as you cook at the end of a long day on the slopes. Some companies will supply you with a timetable of what to do when (especially for young people) but many leave it up to you. If you can design a timetable intuitively then great, but if you can't then follow these steps.

Assume the menu is:

Starter: crispy duck salad with chilli sauce
Main: boeuf bourguignon, dauphinoise potatoes, braised red cabbage, beans
Dessert: chocolate brownies with chocolate sauce

Recipes for all these dishes are in this Bible.

Start by breaking each dish into its steps and assign a time-taken to each step. It's important to remember everything that takes any time at all, e.g. cooling down of hot items before serving. Be generous with your timings as things always take longer than you think and some contingency is needed.

Starter:			**mins.**
Duck Salad	duck	extract from tin	15
		heat	10
		shred	10
		crisp	10
		cool/rest	15
	sauce	make	15
		cool	15
	salad	prep	10
Main course:			
Beef	meat	prepare	20
		cook (1)	180
		add mushrooms	10
		cook (2)	60
Red cabbage	veg	prepare	15
		cook	40
Green beans	veg	cook	10
Dauphinoise	potatoes	prepare	15
		cook (1)	120
		add cheese	5
		cook (2)	15
Dessert:			
Brownies	cake	prepare	20
		cook	30
	sauce	prepare/cook	15
You also need to consider essential tasks like laying the table:			
Miscellany:			
	lay table	cutlery, crockery	10
	last minute	wine, water, bread	5
	serving	warm plates	5

If you were to do each task in order then the whole meal would take about 8 hours! Clearly you can multi-task to bring the time down to something more reasonable – whilst something is cooking you can be preparing something else. But how do you decide what to do when?

For each course:
- ➢ find the item that takes the longest to prepare & cook, e.g. for the starter it is the duck which takes at least 60 mins; for the main it is the beef at over 4 hours
- ➢ working backwards from the time to serve, work out the latest time you must start, e.g. starter is served at 20:00 so you must start at least 60 mins. earlier at about 19:00; allow some contingency
- ➢ fill in all the preparation & cooking steps for the whole course between these start & end times

Also factor in the miscellaneous items like table laying too – they all take time – and you will end up with a timetable like this:

	Starter	**Main**	**Dessert**
15:30		prepare beef	
16:00		cook beef (1)	
17:30		prepare dauphinoise	
17:45		cook dauphinoise (1)	
19:00	extract duck	beef: add mushrooms	
19:15	heat duck	prepare cabbage cook beef (2)	
19:30	shred duck crisp duck make sauce	cook cabbage	
19:45	lay table – cutlery, condiments etc; warm plates & dishes		
19:45	cool/rest duck cool sauce prepare salad	dauphinoise: add cheese	prepare brownies
20:00	lay table – wine, water, bread		
20:00	plate & serve	cook dauphinoise (2) cook beans	cook brownies
20:15		plate & serve	
20:30			make sauce
20:45			plate & serve

It is unlikely that your first attempt at the timetable will be totally successful – it all depends on the menu chosen.

In this example:

> ➤ you have to start work at 15:30 but then you are idle between 17:45 and 19:00
> ➤ between 19:30 and 20:00 you have too much to do
> ➤ after serving the starter at 20:00 you will need to wash-up etc so there's little time to do more preparation

To resolve these issues:

> ➤ do some preparation and cooking in the morning after you have served breakfast; some things like the beef can be cooked in 2 sessions
> ➤ anything that doesn't spoil by prolonged cooking can be started earlier, e.g. red cabbage
> ➤ some things will spoil if started earlier, e.g. beans must be cooked just prior to serving
> ➤ anything that will be served cool can be started earlier, e.g. duck
> ➤ anything that can be re-heated before serving can be started earlier, e.g. chocolate sauce
> ➤ use spare time whilst things are cooking to prepare other things or lay the table etc

By starting some things earlier you will produce a workable time table like this, which you can "tune" after its first use:

	Starter	**Main**	**Dessert**
09:00 to 11:30		prepare & cook beef prepare & cook dauphinoise	
18:30	extract duck make sauce	beef: add mushrooms & cook	
19:00	heat duck		prepare brownies
19:15	shred duck	prepare cabbage	cook brownies
19:30	crisp duck	cook cabbage	make sauce
19:45	lay table – cutlery, condiments etc; warm plates & dishes		
19:45	cool/rest duck & sauce prepare salad	add cheese & cook dauphinoise	
20:00	lay table – wine, water, bread		
20:00	plate & serve	cook beans	
20:15		plate & serve	re-heat sauce
20:45			plate & serve

And of course, you may have to factor in preparing and serving aperitifs and canapes, lighting the chalet fire, and time for socialising with your guests – so leave lots of contingency!

If you're working with someone else in the kitchen then you can annotate each task with the responsible person.

If you're really into project management then you can colour code (or shade/underline etc) who does what. Also the manual prep tasks could be highlighted differently from the cooking periods. This enables you to see at a glance each individual's workload, and also to see what is on the hob and in the oven at any one time (and to see if that's possible to manage).

For example, with 2 kitchen workers (#1 & #2) a segment of your plan may look like this:

19:00	OVEN: heat duck		#1: prepare brownies
19:15	#1: shred duck	#2: prepare cabbage	OVEN: cook brownies
19:30	OVEN: crisp duck	HOB: cook cabbage	#1: prep sauce HOB: cook sauce

Here you can see that no one has too much to do during this period, and the load on the hob and oven looks fine.

TERMINOLOGY & TECHNIQUES

Jeff: *"What does it mean when it says 'roughly chopped onions'; how rough?"*
Anne: *"Well, it's obvious, isn't it?"*

Recipes have their own language – a bit like a quiz, easy if you already know the answer!!

I'm assuming (yes, I know – to assume makes an *ass of you and me*) that you have got some basic cooking experience or at least an interest in the subject. You would probably be foolish to become a chalet host without some elementary culinary skills, so the following definitions, hints and tips might sound a bit condescending. They are included especially for Jeff, and others like him, who knew precious little about cooking when we first took on a chalet. Now he would have no trouble cooking any of these recipes, but he retains the memory of recipes being written in an incomprehensible language with many implicit assumptions.

BASIC

AL DENTE	For pasta, vegetables etc, cooked until it offers a slight resistance to the bite.
BAKE	To cook by dry heat, usually in the oven.
BASTE	To moisten foods during cooking with pan drippings to add flavour and prevent drying.
BEAT	To mix rapidly to make a mixture smooth and light by incorporating lots of air.
BLANCH	To immerse in rapidly boiling water and allow to cook slightly.
BLEND	To incorporate two or more ingredients thoroughly.
BOIL	To heat a liquid until bubbles break continually on the surface.
BROIL	To cook under a grill under strong, direct heat.
CARAMELIZE	To heat sugar in order to turn it brown and give it a special taste.
CREAM	To soften a fat, especially butter, by beating it at room temperature. Butter and sugar are often creamed together, making a smooth, soft paste.
CURE	To preserve meats by drying and salting and/or smoking.
DICE	To cut food in small cubes of uniform size and shape.
DREDGE	To sprinkle or coat with flour or other fine substance.
DRIZZLE	To sprinkle drops of liquid lightly over food in a casual manner.
DUST	To sprinkle food with a dry ingredient, e.g. icing sugar, often using a small sieve.
FILLET	As a verb, to remove the bones from meat or fish. A fillet (or filet) is the piece of flesh after it has been boned.
FLAKE	To break lightly into small pieces.
FLAMBE	To flame foods by dousing in some form of potable alcohol and setting alight.
FOLD	To incorporate a delicate substance, such as whipped cream or beaten egg whites, into another substance without releasing air bubbles, usually using a large metal spoon.
FRY	To cook in hot fat. To cook in a little fat is called pan-frying or sauteing; to cook in a one-to-two inch layer of hot fat is called shallow-fat frying; to cook in a deep layer of hot fat is called deep-fat frying.
GARNISH	To decorate a dish both to enhance its appearance and to provide a flavourful foil.
GRATE	To rub on a grater that separates the food in various sizes of bits or shreds.
GRATIN	From the French word for "crust." Term used to describe any oven-baked dish - usually cooked in a shallow oval gratin dish--on which a golden brown

	crust of bread crumbs, cheese or creamy sauce is formed.
GRILL	To cook under a grill with intense heat.
GRIND	To process solids by hand or mechanically to reduce them to tiny particles.
JULIENNE	To cut vegetables, fruits, or cheeses into thin strips.
KNEAD	To work and press dough with the palms of the hands or mechanically.
LUKEWARM	Neither cool nor warm; approximately body temperature.
MARINATE	To flavour and moisturize pieces of meat, poultry, seafood or vegetable by soaking them in, or brushing them with, a liquid mixture of seasonings known as a marinade. Dry marinade mixtures composed of salt, pepper, herbs or spices may also be rubbed into meat, poultry or seafood.
MEUNIERE	Dredged with flour and sautéed in butter.
MINCE	To cut or chop food into extremely small pieces.
MIX	To combine ingredients usually by stirring.
PAN-BROIL	To cook uncovered in a hot fry pan, pouring off fat as it accumulates.
PAN-FRY	To cook in small amounts of fat.
PARBOIL	To boil until partially cooked; to blanch.
PARE	To remove the outermost skin of a fruit or vegetable.
PEEL	To remove the peels from vegetables or fruits.
PICKLE	To preserve meats, vegetables, and fruits in brine (salt water).
PINCH	A small amount you can hold between your thumb and forefinger.
PIT	To remove pits (stones/seeds) from fruits.
PLUMP	To soak dried fruits in liquid until they swell.
POACH	To cook very gently in hot liquid kept just below the boiling point.
PUREE	To mash foods until perfectly smooth.
REDUCE	To boil down to reduce the volume.
RENDER	To make solid fat into liquid by melting it slowly.
ROAST	To cook by dry heat in an oven.
SAUTE	To cook and/or brown food in a small amount of hot fat.
SCALD	To bring to a temperature just below the boiling point.
SEAR	To brown very quickly by intense heat.
SHRED	To cut or tear in small, long, narrow pieces.
SIMMER	To cook slowly in liquid over low heat. The surface of the liquid should be barely moving, broken from time to time by slowly rising bubbles.
SKIM	To remove impurities, e.g. scum or fat, from the surface of a liquid.
STEEP	To extract colour &/or flavour by leaving in water just below the boiling point.
STERILIZE	To destroy micro organisms by boiling, dry heat, or steam.
STEW	To simmer slowly in a small amount of liquid for a long time.
SWEAT	To cook (usually vegetables) gently so that they soften but do not brown (see later).
TOSS	To combine ingredients with a lifting motion.
TRUSS	To secure poultry with string or skewers, to hold its shape while cooking.
WHIP	For cream or eggs: to beat rapidly to incorporate air (to make bigger).
WHISK	To stir or beat rapidly in order to mix well - with a fork, or hand whisk or electric whisk.

COOKING AT ALTITUDE

It takes a while to get used to being at altitude! The air is thinner and some people find that they get out of breath more easily, have difficulty sleeping, nosebleeds and a dry mouth at night; some even get altitude sickness for a few days. But it is amazing how quickly the human body adapts and you will soon be running up and down those stairs!

Tip: *don't give blood in the UK in the 2 or 3 weeks before you leave for the snow!*

Cooking is different at altitude too. As you go up in altitude, the air gets thinner and the atmospheric pressure drops. Low air pressure has three main effects on cooking:

1. Water boils at a lower temperature.

The result is that it can take longer to cook food, since the chemical and physical reactions that occur during baking and cooking are slower at lower temperatures. At 1500m above sea level, water boils at 95^0C; at 2000m, about 93^0C. The effect of altitude is particularly noticeable when cooking vegetables; for example, cooking a large pan of potatoes for mashing at 2000m can take an hour. Boiled eggs take longer to cook too; you will need to experiment to find the required cooking time at your altitude, but it is in the region of 6 minutes at 2000m for a large egg. To start with, it is best to assume that everything takes longer to cook; allow extra time, especially when boiling is involved.

2. Moisture evaporates more quickly.

At lower pressure, the water molecules can escape more easily, leading to quicker evaporation; this means that:
  - sugar becomes more concentrated which causes cakes and puddings to be more prone to sticking
  - flavours can become weaker, since there are fewer moisture molecules to carry the aromas
  - baked goods tend to dry out and go stale much faster than at sea level.

3. Air bubbles expand and rise more quickly.

Low air pressure induces rapid expansion of leavening gases, which are bubbles formed during baking. As leavening occurs faster, gas bubbles tend to coalesce into large, irregular pockets giving a coarse-textured cake. Alternatively, the pressure inside a rising cake can become so great, that cell walls stretch beyond their maximum and burst, resulting in a dense, flat cake.

As a general guideline for converting your favourite cake/pudding recipes for use at altitude, try using:
  - less sugar and raising agent
  - more liquid, eggs and flour
  - a slightly higher oven temperature.
  - yoghurt in place of milk (the acidity seems to help)

KNIVES & CHOPPING

You can't learn how to chop and slice by reading a book so get someone to show you how to do it safely, or watch the Youtube videos – and practise.

At all times consider what would happen if the knife were to slip... you only have 10 fingers and they have to last 20 weeks so do the maths!
  - Chalet knives have had a rough life so take your own if possible – one large and one small will be adequate, and a good sharpener.
  - Keep your knives very sharp and bizarrely they become safer.
  - Don't leave sharp knives in the washing-up bowl for someone else to find later!
  - Don't put sharp knives in the dishwasher as it blunts them and someone else may not know they're there.
  - Don't chop on work surfaces; it blunts the knife as well as spoiling the surface.
  - Use separate chopping boards for different foodstuffs (see Hygiene section).

- ➤ Keep a supply of blue plasters handy!
- ➤ Finely sliced, when referring to onions & apples etc, means as thin as you can get.
- ➤ Roughly chopped means... just that!

POTS, PANS & DISHES

Selecting the right pan for the recipe can be quite difficult for a newbie cook. Chalets make it easier for you in that the choice is limited to the handful of pots & pans that you'll be supplied with! You won't always have the ideal pan/dish and you'll need to plan which ones to use for each meal to avoid washing up every two minutes.

- ➤ If you're mixing a cake then using a small bowl will mean maximum spillage as you mix the ingredients, whereas too big a bowl will mean maximum wastage as you can't scrape all of the mix out into the baking tin.
- ➤ If the baking tin is too small then the cake might rise and spill over the sides, whereas if it's too big then the cake could end up like a pancake!
- ➤ Some cakes lend themselves to round tins, e.g. coffee cake, whereas others are better presented as loaves, e.g. lemon drizzle.
- ➤ Always use a heavy-bottomed pan for heating milk, porridge etc and use a lowish heat otherwise it will burn, and instead of skiing you'll be scrubbing.
- ➤ Choose a casserole dish that is big enough to hold the meat etc and juices without overflowing.
- ➤ Ramekins are small pots that generally serve one person, e.g. a starter, and come in various sizes so some recipe quantities may need slight adjustment.
- ➤ If you're lucky enough to get a good non-stick pan then keep it just for eggs and never use a metal tool or scourer on it.
- ➤ Don't use plastic utensils in hot pans - sooner or later you'll melt one into your food; many chefs say use only wooden ones.
- ➤ Keep separate wooden utensils for use with savoury things like onions & meats, and delicate flavours like cakes.
- ➤ If you do manage to burn the contents onto the base of a saucepan, e.g. porridge, then scrape out as much of the burnt food as possible using a wooden spatula, then add about an inch of water to the pan with a generous squirt of washing up liquid, and simmer for half-an-hour (do not boil) – then scrape a bit more, and repeat if necessary, and finally apply some elbow grease. You could also try a bio washing powder mixed with water and left to soak.

It's unlikely that your chalet will be equipped with silicon bakeware so take your own if you prefer it, it won't add much to your baggage.

Unfortunately, when it comes to selecting pots/pans to use, there's no substitute for a little common sense and a lot of experience. At least in a chalet you'll be cooking the same dishes time and time again so you should have it pretty perfect by week 3 maybe.

THE OVEN

Virtually all recipes that use an oven require food to be put into a pre-heated oven, so I am mentioning it here and assuming that you can take it as read for each following recipe. Most ovens take about 15 minutes to heat up to 200C. Ovens do vary; the thermostats are not always accurate and can be as much as 20°C out, so you will need to get to know your own oven and adjust temperatures if necessary. Higher shelves in the oven are generally hotter than lower ones. Fan ovens help to overcome this problem and tend to cook more quickly and may need a slightly lower temperature setting.

- ➤ Consider what oven shelves you'll need for the whole meal & arrange accordingly whilst the oven is cold
- ➤ Don't place anything directly on the bottom of the oven as the heating element will overheat the dish; use an upturned cooking tray to make a shelf on the bottom
- ➤ Use oven gloves but beware they may reduce your grip; if they are fabric then don't get them wet as they'll be useless

- Put casseroles, ramekins etc on a baking tray to catch any overflow – it's easier to clean a tray than clean the oven
- Leave plenty space around each dish so that the air can circulate or you'll create hot and cold spots which will impact the cooking times
- Leave plenty of space to allow for pastry, soufflés etc to rise
- When testing to see if a dish is ready, don't leave the oven door open for more than necessary as the oven will cool rapidly and may spoil the dish, e.g. test cakes quickly with a skewer whilst in the oven
- Before removing a hot dish from the oven consider where you'll put it down; don't put hot pans on wooden surfaces – use heatproof mats
- Clean all spillages immediately before they bake on

COOK THOROUGHLY

You don't want to risk giving your guests food poisoning, so be very careful when cooking chicken and pork. Make sure they are thoroughly cooked without a trace of pink; any juices should be clear of blood; if in doubt, use a thermometer which should register 75C or above at the core of the food.

Also, we do not serve raw or partly cooked eggs because of the salmonella risk, it's just not worth the risk (so there are no uncooked soufflés, mousses or baked Alaska in our recipes).

FRYING & SWEATING

When a recipe requires you to fry something, you need to have the pan hot (with oil if required) before adding the food. Do not use a lid and keep the temperature high; usually the food will turn brown when frying. Sweating, on the other hand, is a method of cooking vegetables in a pan, so that they soften but do not brown, in order to bring out their flavour. Use a lower heat setting and cover with a lid. Sometimes salt is added to vegetables when sweating, to draw out the water and prevent browning.

OILS, BUTTER & GREASE

Some people are confused by the different sorts of oils and fats available. And what exactly is grease?

Oil:
- Basically, we only use sunflower and olive oils.
- Sunflower oil is good for anything, e.g. cakes, frying eggs etc.; you'll rarely go wrong if you use it.
- Personally I think that 'vegetable oil' is only good for deep frying, and I never use it. If I find a recipe containing vegetable oil, I substitute sunflower oil.
- Olive oil has more flavour, is more expensive but well worth it, especially for frying meat and for dressings; it's not generally suitable for lightly-flavoured things like cakes.

Lard and margarine are never used in our chalet.

Butter:
- Unsalted butter is best for cooking cakes etc but lightly salted butter is preferable for bread & jam.
- Cut butter into cubes for use on the dinner table as it results in less waste.
- Some cheaper butters are very soft even when refrigerated and won't be easy to cut into cubes for the butter dish but they're fine for cooking.
- Butter can be melted in the microwave: place in a deep dish and give it short bursts (10 seconds) and cover with kitchen roll to contain any spattering.
- When frying with butter, do not use full heat and adding a little oil will reduce the chance of the butter burning. If it does burn then clean the pan thoroughly and start again otherwise the taste will seriously mar the food!

Grease:

- Where a recipe says "grease" a dish it means coat the dish with a fine layer of oil or butter (as appropriate to the recipe) using kitchen roll as a wipe. This reduces the chance of the food sticking to the dish.
- When cooking cakes, it's worth dusting the greased (buttered) baking tin with flour too but ensure all excess flour is removed by tapping the tin upside down. This helps to release the cake from the tin when cooled.
- Often cake tins are lined with a good quality non-stick baking parchment as well to help the cake release (at least the bottom of the tin is lined, the sides are often too much of a fiddle).

MEASURING

The first time you try a new recipe then I suggest you measure every ingredient carefully with scales but after a while you will learn quicker ways to measure and that some things can be *guess-timated*.

Many ingredients are not critical and if you are within 10% the recipe will probably still be fine: for instance, for a cake recipe, eggs can be quite small through to quite large, so the flour can similarly be slightly more or less. You will learn how to guess many ingredients (and which ones are crucial to weigh). However, spices and seasonings should always be treated with respect and you should err on the lower side of the amount needed until you've tried tasting it – you can't remove salt once it's added!

Some measuring tips etc:
- mechanical scales are generally not very accurate for small weights (under 100g); try "bouncing" the scales a few times to get an average reading
- electronic scales are very precise and can often be zeroed as you add each ingredient (so your maths doesn't get taxed)
- invest in a measuring jug that has dry measures for sugar, flour etc
- a teaspoon, abbreviated to *tsp*, holds 5ml so it's a volume not a weight, and when referring to water it's also 5g; but not all teaspoons in the cutlery drawer are the same so use a graduated one where possible; a level teaspoon refers to a volume of powder, e.g. sugar, that exactly fills the spoon and is 5ml (but not 5g!); a rounded teaspoon refers to powder which is piled up a bit and a heaped spoon is piled up a bit more – both are unspecific in terms of quantity!
- a tablespoon, abbreviated *tbsp*, holds 15ml and has similar variations as the teaspoon
- butter packets are often marked in 25g portions, or you can divide a 250g pack by eye into half, then half again etc
- a portion of rice is about 1 small handful or 1 espresso cupful
- a portion of spaghetti is a bunch about 20-25mm (about 1 inch) diameter
- for items in small packets you can often guess the needed amount by eye, knowing the weight of a full packet, e.g. raisins, chocolate
- for bulk measures like porridge, flour & sugar, you may find that the amount needed is that held by a cup or a mug or an empty tin, so measure once and thereafter use a cup/mug for speed
- weighing syrups/treacles is difficult as it sticks to the spoon, so put the treacle tin on the scales and spoon out the treacle until the weight has reduced by the appropriate amount then ensure you use the spoon to mix well and use all the treacle on the spoon; lightly greasing the spoon allows the treacle etc to run off more easily.

Some handy measures, in grams, from which you can *guess-timate* almost anything (note, the pot measure is a standard small 125g yoghurt pot):

	Level teaspoon	Level tablespoon	½ Level Pot	Level Pot
water	5	15	~60	~120
flour	3	10	~40	~75
sugar (any sort)	5	15	~60	~120
oats	-	-	~35	~70
sultanas/raisins	-	-	~45	~90
rice	-	-	~55	~110

SCALING

All recipes are designed for a certain number of servings; those in this book are for 8 people (unless specifically stated). If your chalet has 12 beds then it's worth scaling up all the recipes (that you may use) once at the start of the season, rather than doing the mental juggling every week when you cook the recipe. Sometimes your chalet is not full, or an extra guest arrives for a meal, and then you'll just have to do the maths on the fly!

In general, scaling up (or down) is simply a question of increasing (or decreasing) all ingredients by the required ratio, e.g. using our recipes, if you have 12 guests then you'll need to increase all ingredients by 12/8, i.e. 1.5; so 4 eggs becomes 6 eggs, 200g of flour becomes 300g, etc. If the recipe calls for 3 eggs then you'll have to use some common sense and scale up to either 4 or 5 eggs and scale everything else accordingly.

Bear in mind, when scaling up:
> don't underestimate the increased preparation time for some recipes, e.g. those involving chopping or searing meat
> bigger pots/pans will take longer to come to the boil; you may be better off using 2 or more pots/pans as they'll come to the boil quicker
> bear in mind a large pot/pan will be very heavy
> don't overfill pots/pans as any spillage will give you more work
> using a bigger pot/pan may mean that one of your hob rings, or part of an oven shelf, is no longer available so your whole menu may no longer be workable!
> 1 very large cake may cook on the outside but be still uncooked on the inside, so 2 cakes may be better; it's also difficult to get more than 8 to 10 pieces out of a round cake no matter how big it is, so loaf cakes may work better

Bear in mind, when scaling down:
> remember to scale down any seasoning or spices as they'll have a more marked influence
> go easy on thickeners like cornflour as they may turn your gravy to jelly quite quickly
> consider using a smaller tin for cakes otherwise it may turn out quite flat

SEASONING, HERBS & SPICES

Lots of recipes say "season to taste" but what does that mean? A seasoning is an ingredient that improves the flavour and possibly the appearance of a dish, either by enhancing the natural flavours of other ingredients, or by adding its own flavour.

Normally, seasoning simply means adding salt &/or pepper (and possibly other herbs and spices) until *you* think it tastes OK. Always bear in mind that someone else's taste will differ from yours and err on the cautious side. Guests can add more salt later but they can't take it out.

Salt is almost essential in savoury dishes. Our taste buds have evolved to need it. Imagine mashed potatoes with no salt – ugh! But many ingredients have natural salt in them so may not need more added, e.g. a recipe using lardons (bacon) is unlikely to need further salt. We don't add salt routinely to many dishes in case the health-police catch us and many guests are now anti-salt!

We use black pepper, which we grind as needed, quite a lot, e.g. for enhancing soups. Don't overdo it as some people don't like anything peppery – they can always add more.

The use of herbs and spices to my mind is one thing that separates cooks from chefs. I (Jeff) add these as per the recipe and I might add a bit extra if I don't think the taste is strong enough but I wouldn't know what substitutions I could make if I was out of stock; but Anne will say "use a bit of that instead".

The difference between a herb and a spice relates to their source; they both come from plants; herbs from the leafy part; and spices from the stem or root or fruit or nut of a plant.

Common herbs used in chalet cooking are: parsley, basil, thyme, bay, rosemary and mint. These are best bought fresh each week if possible but dried varieties are available too as a back-up.

Common spices used in the chalet are: cinnamon, cloves, ginger, vanilla and nutmeg. These are generally bought in their dried form and are quite strong so use with care. We also keep dried garlic as a back up in case we run out of fresh.

Successful seasoning is a bit of an art form so stick to the recipes initially and experiment cautiously.

RICE

Rice used for dinner (with curry etc) has a long grain. The best sort is called Basmati rice.
Risotto rice has a shorter grain and is usually known as Arborio rice.
Pudding rice is very short grained.

Cooks, chefs and mere mortals have all sorts of favourite ways of cooking 'perfect' rice. Mine was shown to me by a Thai student when I was a teenager, and it has served me well ever since.

Half fill a saucepan with boiling water, add a pinch of salt and about 50g (a small handful) rice per person. Bring to the boil, stir well, put a lid on the pan and reduce the heat to a simmer. Cook for 11 minutes (or slightly longer at altitude), then taste to make sure it is soft.
Drain through a colander and rinse with plenty of boiling water (you may find it easier to return the rice to the pan and swill it around in the boiling water. Drain again, then place the colander, covered with a clean tea towel or lid, over a pan of barely simmering water for a few minutes.

Tip: Rice should be served straight away (well, fairly quickly) and not left to stand as it contains bacterial spores that are not always killed by boiling water. These will turn into poisonous bacteria if left. If you cool cooked rice quickly by dowsing with cold water then it can be kept in a covered container in the fridge for no more than 1 day. Re-heat it thoroughly by placing in a colander over boiling water until it's piping hot all the way through. Never re-heat more than once.

PASTA

Half fill a large saucepan with boiling water; bring to a fast boil before adding the pasta and keep the water boiling without a lid on the pan. Italians like to say that the cooking water should be as salty as sea water, although that is not popular with the health police. The pasta must be well covered with water so that it has plenty of room to move around. Give it a stir and then cook, without a lid, for the time recommended on the packet, drain well and serve immediately. Pasta should be cooked *al dente,* with a bit of bite.
As a general rule, allow about 100g pasta per adult for a main course.

THICKENING SAUCES

Some recipes instruct you to **reduce** the sauce or stock. This simply means you simmer the sauce and allow some of the water (maybe half) to evaporate, thus concentrating the taste of the remaining sauce as well as thickening it.

Where a sauce doesn't need concentrating but does need thickening, then **cornflour** is often used.
Care: you must use it properly to prevent the sauce tasting grainy or going lumpy.
Mix a tablespoon of cornflour with 2-3 tablespoons of <u>cold</u> water until you have a smooth paste; this is known as *slaking*. This can then be added *slowly* to hot liquids; stir well and simmer for a few minutes to thicken.
The quantity of cornflour required will vary. As a very rough guide, 1 tablespoon of cornflour when slaked and added to half a litre of gravy/sauce stock will give a thickish sauce.
Add it a bit at a time; you can always add more but you can't take it out! If you do make a sauce too thick, add extra liquid, hot or cold, mix well and simmer for a few minutes.

ROUX SAUCE

Some recipes require you to make a *roux* sauce. A roux is basically a cooked blend of fat and flour, which is used as a thickening agent.
To make a basic white sauce (i.e. a roux based on milk), melt 50g butter in a pan and get it *frothing* but not boiling. Add 50g plain flour and cook gently for 2-3 minutes, stirring constantly, until the mixture forms a smooth paste. Add milk a bit (say 50ml) at a time, stirring constantly and allowing the mixture to gently boil, forming a smooth paste, between additions. For a thick sauce, you will need about 300ml milk. Continue adding milk until the sauce is the right consistency.
Various ingredients can then be added to this basic sauce, e.g. tomato puree, cheese.
Tip: *use a big pan as it's amazing how the mix expands; use one that holds at least three times the volume of milk; heating the milk (perhaps in a microwave) almost to boiling before use gives a faster and better mix. A cheat's roux sauce can be made by thickening cream with slaked corn flour!*

CHOCOLATE

For optimum flavour, when dark chocolate is used in cooking, it should contain at least 70% cocoa solids.
Chocolate needs to be melted carefully. We usually do it in the microwave, but it is very easy to overheat and burn it. Break the chocolate into small pieces and place in a non metallic bowl (make sure that no foil gets in with the chocolate!) Microwave on medium power in short bursts, checking and stirring frequently until smooth.
A safer, but slower method is to place the bowl over a pan containing a little simmering water, stirring until melted.

EGGS

A chalet for 10 people will use 100+ eggs a week! They take up a lot of space but there's no need to keep these in the fridge as they'll be fine at room temperature; just ensure you use the oldest ones first. They come in trays of 20-30 and old trays make excellent heat-mats or fire kindling. *However, in Austria the rule is that eggs MUST be kept in the fridge.*

CREAM

Most chalet companies use long life cream, which comes in litre packs like long-life milk, and is widely available in French supermarkets. For whipping, you need a high fat content (preferably at least 35 %). Some of the cream sold for whipping has a lower fat content and this will take ages to whip. Chill cream in the fridge before whipping. Whipping creates a lot of spatter; to minimise the mess, use a high sided container and cover the top with a plastic bag (taking care not to get it wrapped around the whisk).

Crème fraiche is a French type of sour cream, with a fat content of about 28%. It is particularly useful in finishing sauces because it does not curdle when cooked. However, "light" crème fraiche with a low fat content curdles when heated.

ONIONS

Many recipes tell you to "peel, chop and fry an onion". This may only take ten minutes but minutes add up to lost ski time. We make a large batch of "onion base", i.e. about 1 kg of onions: peeled, chopped & fried until soft but not too brown, perhaps once a week when the guests aren't around to smell it, and store it in pots in the fridge. You can also buy frozen onions that are already peeled and sliced and we don't think you can tell the difference in most recipes. When a recipe calls for one onion then simply substitute about a tablespoon of onion base. And no washing up!

CHEESE

France is famous for its cheeses, but in our opinion its hard cheeses are not a patch on Cheddar, which is expensive and not widely available in France. The standard cheese used for cooking is Emmental, which is available grated (*rapê*) and in blocks. It has a very mild flavour.
Gruyere is an alternative hard cheese with a stronger flavour, but it is relatively expensive.
For cooking, we tend to use a mixture of grated Emmental with grated Parmesan for flavour.

FLOUR

There are essentially two types of flour of interest in chalet cooking: plain and self-raising (SR); the latter has a *raising agent* added that makes the cake/pudding/pastry rise up during baking, but the same effect can be achieved by using plain flour and adding your own raising agent to the mix.

Raising agent is bought in sachets, usually of 11g which is 3 level teaspoons (a handy measure for cakes), or can be found in bigger tubs which is more economical but requires measuring each time. It works by releasing carbon dioxide when it reacts with the acidity of the mix and the heat. Sometimes it's referred to as *baking powder,* and you may come across recipes that use *bicarbonate of soda* as a raising agent.

In the UK, plain flour and self-raising flour are both easily available and cost about the same.

In France there are many types of flour: *Farine de ble - t*ype 55 is general multipurpose white plain flour. *Farine gateaux* is similar to self raising flour, with a slightly lower proportion of raising agent (*levure chimique*) and is relatively expensive.

To convert plain flour to self raising, add 3 level teaspoons, i.e. 1 sachet, of raising agent to each 250g flour.

Our recipes use only plain flour with raising agent as needed.

If a recipe includes raising agent, cooking must follow mixing without undue delay, as the raising agent starts to react as soon as it is mixed with liquid.

PASTRY

Chalet hosts don't make pastry (phew, that's good!) – they use ready-made pastry that in France comes as a rolled-up circle ideally sized to fit a large flan tin. In the UK the pastry tends to be square – why?

You'll come across two types: short-crust pastry (brisee -sweetened or sable-unsweetened) which doesn't rise very much, and flaky pastry (feuilletee) which rises and cooks to give a myriad of brittle overlapping flakes. Puff pastry is similar to flaky but is manufactured to give multiple uniform layers rather than separate flakes. Use whatever sort suits the dish that you are preparing.

Note that some pastry is made with lard which is not eaten by vegetarians and vegans.

Tip: *Take pastry out of fridge 15 minutes before it's needed otherwise it may crack when unrolled, but not too early or it goes sticky!*

Recipes sometimes require you to 'bake blind', which doesn't mean that you simply close your eyes, it means you bake the pastry initially without any filling in it, so that it turns out crisp and does not go soggy from the wet filling, which is added prior to a second bake. Pastry tends to rise up as it cooks, unless it is weighted down. You can merely push it down with a fork afterwards; this is the method we use for small patty (fairy cake) tins. For larger tins, you can get special ceramic beans to weight down the pastry, but we have always used rice. Any sort will do, and you can save it when cooled in a plastic bag or jar, for use time and time again. To bake blind:

- Line your tin with pastry, and prick all over with a fork
- Cover the pastry with non-stick baking parchment, then pour on enough rice to completely cover the paper
- Cook in a pre-heated oven at 200C for about 10 minutes until it's golden but not yet brown
- Remove the rice and paper and cook for a further 5 minutes; remember it will be cooked again with the filling so don't overcook it at this stage.

Instead of making "boring" round pastry cases for a canapé or starter, try these fancy square ones – dead easy to impress:

- cut out a square of pastry
- cut right through the pastry as shown by dotted lines; do not join all the corners
- fold opposite corners A-to-B and B-to-A, one going under the other
- overlap the folded parts with the edge of the dotted square and press gently to seal
- you'll end up with a small "tray" with 2 twisted corners – very impressive when cooked

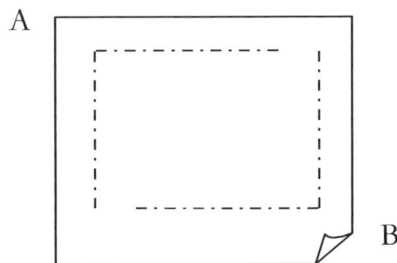

PREPARING TO COOK

- ➢ Assemble all the necessary ingredients while your hands are clean
- ➢ Assemble all the bowls/pots/spoons/baking tins etc that you'll need
- ➢ As you add each ingredient to the mix move the packet to one side then if you're interrupted you'll know what's in the mix & what's not
- ➢ It's not necessary to weigh each ingredient individually and place in separate bowls before you mix them all together (as the TV chefs do) – think of all that washing up! – simply weigh one ingredient then add it to the mix before doing the next
- ➢ When separating egg yolks & whites separate each egg individually before adding it to the mix else a single mistake spoils the whole mix

WHILE YOU'RE COOKING

➢ Use a timer – it's so easy to forget what's cooking
➢ Peer in the glass oven door rather than opening it, until the dish is looking nearly ready
➢ Check often that everything you need to cook is being cooked, or is ready to cook. Even we have forgotten the peas or rice on occasions!

AFTER COOKING

➢ Allow dishes/pots to cool slightly then rinse with water so they'll be easier to wash-up (take care with cast-iron pots that may shatter if plunged into cold water!)
➢ Don't pour fat/oil down the sink unless you're intent on blocking it up! Pour warm fat into an old tin where it may solidify, or add used paper towel & serviettes to the tin to soak up the fat
➢ Keep used (but clean) serviettes for general cleaning of spillages & wiping fat from pans

RECIPES

All the recipes in this book have been tried and tested at altitude; they are easy and they work; they all serve 8 guests (except for the recipes for children and special dietary requirements, which each serves the number stated).

Preparation time

We haven't included preparation times as they're of little value. Some people can chop a carrot in seconds whereas others take ages. You know yourself if you're a speedy worker or a bit of a plodder. The first time you try a recipe you shouldn't rush; re-read it several times; assemble the ingredients first then work methodically; and give yourself plenty of prep time. As you cook each recipe week after week you will speed up significantly.

Cooking time

The stated cooking times are a guide at 1500 metres altitude; actual times may vary depending on your cooker/oven, pot-size, altitude, and sometimes even the type of ingredients.

Test the dish several minutes before times-up - it may be done already or need even longer!

N.B.

We have not included dozens of glossy photos in this book. This is partly to minimise production costs but also because the recipes will serve as "reminders" to chalet hosts rather than strict "how-tos". Also, one photo doesn't show any complicated steps that a recipe may have.

You can find photos & videos of many of the recipes in this book at www.cococookery.co.uk/foodpics/.

BREAKFASTS

Skiers (and boarders) appreciate a good breakfast before setting off for the slopes for the day. They use a lot of energy during the day and need to stock up on calories before they go out.

Breakfast time can be fairly hectic, particularly if any of the guests have morning lessons, (and you're perhaps not at your best?) so it really does pay to be organised.

Unlike evening dinner which is at a fixed time, guests may arrive for breakfast in twos and threes or en masse, at any time between say 8am and 9am. Some may want just cereals and some may want everything that's going. In my view, every guest deserves a hot fresh breakfast and not a dried up fried egg cooked 30 minutes ago.

If you are able to, it is much easier to restrict the available breakfast to a single cooked option; say bacon, fried eggs and mushrooms one day; sausage, scrambled egg and baked beans the next. If you are expected to offer every option freshly cooked each morning, you may find that you run out of hob space, and the guests have to wait a long time for their breakfasts. One way of dealing with this is to precook bacon, sausages, tomatoes, mushrooms etc, and keep them warm in the oven. On the down side, the food will not be as good it would be freshly cooked, and there may be a lot of waste. It also puts fat in your oven so more cleaning is needed to avoid bacon-flavoured cakes!

General tips for breakfast:
- If you are able to lay up the table the previous night, it will save you time in the morning, but often guests like to sit around the dinner table for hours, and you can't turf them off!
- If your dishwasher has a quick cycle then wash up last night's left over glasses etc immediately.
- It's definitely worth ensuring you have enough milk/juice/eggs/cereals/jams etc before you finish for the night to avoid an early morning panic.
- Keep frying pans warm on a very low heat at all times so you can respond quickly to guests' arrival.
- If parents are stressing over little Johnny's lost goggles then be helpful but don't go looking for the demon goggles; stick to your kitchen and concentrate on breakfast or chaos will ensue with burnt porridge and other frustrated guests.
- Clean out frying pans frequently with kitchen roll (or used but clean serviettes) during cooking to remove burnt butter & oil.
- If you have spare time waiting for guests to arrive then assemble the ingredients for the afternoon cake but be wary of actually starting to cook it unless the bulk of your breakfasts have been served – otherwise for sure, everything will happen at once. You could also prep vegetables for the evening meal.
- Warm the plates for cooked options, including porridge.

Laying the breakfast table:
- Cutlery (knife, fork & spoon) can be laid out bistro-style, maybe wrapped in a serviette.
- Each place will also need a side plate and water (or fruit juice) glass.
- Egg cups & teaspoons can be placed in the middle of the table.
- Salt and pepper, ketchup, sauces in their bottles.
- Sugar (brown and white) in ramekins.
- Cut butter into cubes and serve in a ramekin.
- Serve jams & honey in ramekins or small clean jars with spoons; honey is fine in a squeezy bottle; nutella is popular too.
- Serve milk and fruit juices in jugs.
- A jug of water needs to be ice cold, maybe with a slice of lemon.
- Bread: baguette cut in chunks in a basket, or on a board for guests to cut their own.

➢ Cereals are best left out for guests to help themselves, maybe in plastic containers; with bowls stacked nearby.

➢ Yoghurts can be kept cool by standing in a bowl of iced water or snow!

➢ We think coffee should be freshly made from ground coffee in a cafetiere (or coffee machine), although some guests prefer instant which is much easier for you. We do also keep instant decaff against our better judgement! It's best if the host prepares the coffee-maker as guests can be messy!

➢ Teapot, kettle, mugs, teabags & teaspoons can be left on a side table for guests to make tea just as they like it.

➢ Fruit bowl - check and replenish as necessary.

➢ Use a side table for cereals etc if the table is too small.

PORRIDGE

Porridge is often popular; it can be made in the microwave, but if several of your guests want porridge, it is much better made slowly in a pan.

Single servings can be made in the microwave but I find the results a little unpredictable and unsatisfactory. Sometimes it turns out like wallpaper paste! But here goes: mix 1/3rd mug of oats with about 2/3rd mug of milk and microwave for an initial 2 minutes, stir, then cook for a further minute; stand for a couple of minutes before serving.

For a pan-full to serve 8: mix two mugfuls (about 250g) of oats with 1 ½ litres of milk in a large heavy-based saucepan. Heat very, very slowly, stirring from time to time, until the mixture comes to the boil. Don't be tempted to turn up the heat or the bottom will burn and the porridge will taste awful. It will take about half an hour, then turn right down to barely simmering. Extra milk or oats can be added to adjust the consistency. Keep topping it up with extra milk and oats as required. Serve in warm bowls.

Guests can add demerara sugar or honey, or even salt - heaven forbid. One Danish guest even added butter!

Adding a cinnamon stick (not a crumbly one) to the saucepan gives the porridge a nice spicy kick.

If we have porridge afficiandos staying then we sometimes make a special 'off-piste' version by adding fruit and nuts e.g. raspberries and slivered almonds, raisins and walnuts; part-cream & part milk; occasionally with a dash of whisky.

It's tricky knowing how much porridge to cook on the first day with new guests – too much and it's wasted, too little and you've got to quickly rustle up more for eager skiers. On the first evening we ask our guests for a rough idea of who wants it, then it's easy to make a bit more as you serve by adding milk & oats to the pan on-the-fly.

If anyone has a great idea for using left-over chalet porridge then please tell us – we've tried all sorts of things but nothing really works. It's probably good for filling up the gaps in someone's loose ski boots!

CROISSANTS

Croissants are often served in the chalet. If you're lucky they are delivered by the baker each day, although this will hit your budget big-time! Frozen ones are excellent, as are *pain au chocolat:* get them out of the freezer the night before and leave at room temperature to rise, then about ten minutes in hot oven (200 C) should do it. Some frozen ones can be cooked from the freezer with good results.

They are nice coated with apricot jam before cooking – simply warm a spoonful or two of the jam in the microwave and brush over the pastries.

SCRAMBLED EGGS

Allow about 1½ eggs per person (depending on what else is being served).
Add a tablespoon of milk (or cream) per person to the eggs in a jug and mix well with a fork.
Add a little freshly ground pepper.
Cook over medium heat in a little melted butter in a non stick pan, stirring constantly until scrambled.
Serve with sprig of fresh parsley to impress.
Serve with smoked salmon for a taste of luxury.
Tips: Don't add salt until after cooking or it will give a grey tinge – or leave the guests to add their own!

BOILED EGGS

Immerse eggs into boiling water and boil for about 4½-6 minutes for a medium soft egg. You will need to experiment to find the best timing for your altitude. Occasionally, the eggs crack and some egg-white escapes and cooks in the water; simply scoop this out and discard it; the egg will be fine unless it's actually exploded!
Tips: Only add about half a dozen eggs to a medium-sized pan of water otherwise its temperature will drop markedly and your timings will be way off. Using two pans allows you to cope with guests arriving for breakfast at different times. Use a marker pen to mark eggs that are placed in the pan later than others to allow a production line of eggs, e.g. +1 (minute), +2.

FRIED EGGS

Crack the egg into hot oil and immediately scoop any runaway white back towards the main mass. Leave alone to cook for a few minutes then use a spatula to ensure it's not sticking. Splash surplus oil over egg to cook the topside. It's cooked when there's no raw white to be seen and ideally the bottom is crispy.
Some people like it flipped over & some don't.
You can cook several in the pan at once.
Tips: Test if oil is hot by dropping a tiny droplet of water into the pan – it should sizzle. Do not crack eggs on the side of the frying pan as egg white will drip down side of pan and harden on the hob, which is a pain to clean.

POACHED EGGS

Fill a large frying pan ¾ full of water and get it boiling rapidly. Add a capful of vinegar as this helps to bind the egg white. Place a ring (a pastry cutter works well but silicone alternatives are preferable) in the pan and crack the egg into the ring; as soon as it starts to set around the edges (maybe half a minute), remove the ring with a twisting action and leave the egg until cooked (usually about 4 minutes). Splash hot water over the top to give a nice cooked white finish. You can cook several in the pan at once.

OUEFS EN PAIN

Slice a baguette diagonally about 2cm thick; remove centre dough to leave a ring of crust. Fry the ring lightly in butter on both sides until golden brown, then crack an egg into the centre. If any egg white escapes let it cook slightly then flip it onto top of bread. Then flip the whole bread/egg combo carefully to cook both sides leaving the centre egg runny. You can cook several in the pan at once.
Tips: You can use yesterday's old bread. You can fry the bread rings at any time and set aside until the guests arrive. As you crack the egg, press down on the bread slightly to minimise egg white leakage.

FRENCH TOAST

Known as "Pain Perdu" in France (lost bread); and as eggy bread in UK!
Make up a scrambled egg mix as above and cut slices of baguette diagonally about 2cm thick. Each egg will serve about three slices. Put the mixture in a wide shallow dish and soak the bread in the mixture for about a half-a-minute each side. Fry in butter for about 2 minutes each side until golden. You can cook several in the pan at once.
A nice variation is to coat each slice in a mix of sugar & cinnamon before frying.

Tips: *You can use yesterday's old bread. After placing in pan, pour a dessertspoon of the egg mixture onto each slice to ensure there is egg all the way through the dough.*

BACON & SAUSAGES

Fry in oil in a fairly hot pan, turning every few minutes.
Bacon shrinks enormously and often oozes water and takes only a few minutes each side. Some people like it crispy and some not.
Sausages take five minutes or so if fresh, or around fifteen minutes from frozen. Pricking them with a fork a few times before cooking will help prevent them from splitting.

TOMATOES, BEANS & MUSHROOMS

Mushrooms can be sliced thickly or cut into quarters depending on size, and fried in butter or micro-waved in a bowl with butter; either way takes only a few minutes.

Fresh tomatoes can be sliced thickly and fried in oil for a few minutes. Alternatively, cut in half and bake in oven on a tray for about 15 minutes.

Tinned tomatoes and baked beans just need bringing up to the boil in a saucepan; or in a bowl in the micro-wave when it's best to cover the bowl with kitchen roll to prevent splattering your nice clean oven.

French baked beans are foul but can be made more palatable by adding tomato puree, Worcester sauce and brown sugar – best to go for Heinz!

APPLE RINGS

Remove the core from an eating apple, and slice into rings with a hole in the middle.
Mix some brown sugar and ground cinnamon in a saucer.
Dip each slice in the spicy sugar then fry in butter till golden.

PANCAKES (CREPES)

Makes about 10 thin, French-style pancakes.
Serve with sugar and lemon quarters; chocolate spread (Nutella) is popular too; or fill with ham and grated cheese.

300g plain flour
pinch salt
4 large eggs
about 500ml milk
1 tbsp melted butter

Sift flour into bowl, add salt.
Make a well in the centre; crack in the eggs and start mixing in the flour with a wooden spoon.
Add milk slowly; mixing aggressively with the spoon to blend, until the consistency is like single cream.
Transfer the mix to a jug for ease of pouring into pan.

Mix in melted butter just before cooking (be careful if you have left the mixture in the fridge overnight as the butter tends to solidify instantly on meeting the cold liquid!)
Lightly grease a non-stick frying pan with butter, heat until a small knob of butter sizzles!
Pour in 2-3 tablespoons of mixture; swirl around to coat the pan thinly.
Once the underside is golden (the edges will start to curl away from the pan), flip and cook the other side.
For some reason, the first pancake I cook always seems to turn out wrong, so I discard it!
Serve on warmed plates, perhaps by folding twice into quarters.
Kids may be amused by your flipping skills – even more so when you drop one.

Tips: *Wipe frying pan with kitchen-roll & add small knob of butter, now & again.*
The mixture benefits from resting for a while before use (for best results make overnight and store in the fridge but add the butter in the morning). You can make these in advance and simply re-heat by flashing them in a hot frying pan for a minute or so before serving. They can also be frozen after cooking & re-heat as above after thawing.

AMERICAN PANCAKES

These are the thicker, smaller, sweet pancakes, usually served with maple syrup. The mixture should be prepared immediately before cooking because it uses a raising agent.

Makes about 20
350 g plain flour
3 tsp raising agent
4 tbsp sugar
3 eggs
1 tbsp melted butter
About 100 ml milk

Sift flour and raising agent into a bowl, stir in sugar with wooden spoon.
Make a well in the centre; add eggs and mix with spoon.
Gradually mix in enough milk to form a smooth thick batter.
Mix in the melted butter.

Drop a large spoonful onto a hot greased pan and cook until bubbles appear and the pancake changes from glossy to dull.
Turn and cook for another minute.
You can cook several at once.

For apple pancakes add one eating apple, peeled, cored and grated with ½ tsp cinnamon to the mix.
For savoury omit the sugar and serve with crispy bacon.

Tips: *Wipe frying pan with kitchen-roll & add small knob of butter, now & again.*
You can make these in advance and simply re-heat by flashing them in a hot frying pan for a minute or so before serving. They can also be frozen after cooking & re-heat as above after thawing.
Use surplus mixture to make blinis for canapés.

CAKES

Cakes cook <u>very</u> differently at high altitude, and you may find that your favourite recipes from home just don't turn out very well. The following recipes have all been tried and tested at altitude.

Each recipe serves at least 8 people. If you are making larger cakes, you may need to increase the baking time a little.

There are a few simple rules which apply to all the cake recipes:

➤ Collect all ingredients and equipment before you start to mix.
➤ Grease cake tins (use a piece of kitchen roll with a little sunflower oil), dust with flour and line with non-stick baking parchment (always line the bottom, sometimes it's too tricky to line the sides); this all helps to release the cake when cooked. Cut out a half-dozen liners at a time by folding the paper and cutting just once and then store them flat between baking tins.
➤ Preheat oven (turn on before mixing the cakes).
➤ Cakes containing raising agent (or self raising flour) must be cooked as soon as they are mixed.
➤ Generally, there is no need to sift flour as you'll use it so quickly that it doesn't sit long enough in your store to form clumps. But if you've got a *claggy* bag then sieve it.
➤ Ordinary white granulated sugar (*cristal*) is a bit too coarse for some recipes; caster sugar (poudre) is more expensive but gives a better result.
➤ Use demerera (*cassonade*) where it calls for brown sugar; the recipes will specifically state soft-brown sugar (*vergeoise brune*) where definitely needed.
➤ To test whether a cake is done, pierce with a skewer or small knife; if the cake is cooked the skewer will come out clean. Usually when cakes are done they will spring back when pushed gently on top, and they often shrink slightly away from the sides of the tin.
➤ Remove cakes from the tin as soon as possible and allow to cool on a cooling rack before icing.

YOGHURT CAKES

Yoghurt cakes are a chalet staple; simple to make and virtually foolproof; infinitely variable with the addition of alternative flavourings. The following basic recipe is suitable for a large loaf tin (about 28x10cm) or a large (about 24cm) round or square tin. There is no need to weigh anything, simply use the yoghurt pot (standard 125g size) to measure the ingredients.

1 pot plain yoghurt
1 pot caster sugar
4 eggs
1 pot sunflower oil
 4 pots plain flour
1 sachet (11g) raising agent

Place all ingredients in a large bowl & beat well, ensuring that the mixture is very smooth.
Spoon the mix into the prepared tin & bake for about **30 minutes at 180C** if using a round or square tin, about 45 mins for a loaf tin.
Allow to cool slightly before turning out onto a cooling rack.

Icing:

Icings and fillings made from butter and cream are inadvisable in a chalet as the cake will often be standing in a warm chalet for many hours and the cream can go off. For a basic icing that suits many cakes, melt a 1cm cube of butter in a small pan with a little (2-3 tbsp) warm water; mix in about 150g sifted icing sugar until the icing is thick enough not to run too easy but not so thick that it can't be spread over the cake; spread over the cooled cake and use a palette knife to smooth (dip it frequently in hot water if the icing begins to set); you won't achieve a perfect flat finish with this icing but it's quick and easy so go for a snow scene effect. This basic icing can be adapted to suit various cakes – see below.

The following cakes are all variations on the basic yoghurt recipe above.

Simple sponge cake

Add 1 tsp vanilla essence to the mix.
When cool, slice the cake in half, sandwich together with jam and sprinkle with icing sugar.
Alternatively, use the basic icing with a few drops of vanilla essence.

Lemon drizzle cake

Use a loaf tin.
Add the grated zest of 2 lemons and juice of one lemon to the mix and then cook.
Mix the juice of a lemon with about 100g granulated sugar before the cake is cooked.
When cooked, make small holes all over the top with a skewer then pour the lemon/sugar mix all over.
Allow to cool completely before turning out of the tin.
Optionally, slice the cake in two and sandwich with home-made lemon curd (see Lemon Tart recipe).

Date and walnut loaf

Use a loaf tin.
Add 100g chopped dates and 50g chopped walnuts to the mix.

Chocolate cake

This makes a good birthday cake! It can also be used as a dessert – serve with pouring cream or hot chocolate sauce.

Use a round tin.

Replace 1 pot flour with 1 pot cocoa powder.

Allow cake to cool completely before icing.

Use the basic icing but add about 30g cocoa and mix well – you'll probably need a bit more water too; spread over the cake and decorate before the icing sets (grated white chocolate, vermicelli or smarties, chocolate buttons, hundreds and thousands etc if the cake is for a child's birthday).

Coffee and walnut smiley cake

Use a round tin.

Add 2 tbsp cooled coffee to the mix (and some chopped walnuts as well if you like).

For the icing, use warm strong black coffee instead of water in the basic icing then use walnut pieces to make a smiley face.

Marmalade cake

Use a round tin.

Add 1 pot of marmalade or orange jam to the mix.

Remove the zest from an orange then use the juice (instead of water) to make a flavoured basic icing; ice the cake then decorate with the zest.

Apple and cinnamon cake

Use a square tin.

Add 2 tsps cinnamon powder and 2 chopped apples (peeled, cored and in 1cm chunks) to the mix; sprinkle with demerara sugar before baking. Cut into squares when cool.

Alternatively use a loaf tin.

Coconut ski cake

Use a round tin.

Replace 1 pot flour with desiccated coconut.

When cool, cut cake in half horizontally and sandwich back together with jam.

Use basic icing and sprinkle generously with desiccated coconut to create an authentic snow scene!

Now get creative and fashion a *Silver Skier* (or snowboarder) from cocktail sticks, bag ties and silver foil to go on top of the "snow". Last year our skier lasted the whole season with a little surgery now and again, until a little girl asked to take him home with her!

Carrot and ginger cake

Use a round tin.

Replace the white sugar with soft brown sugar.

Add a large grated carrot, 2 tsp ground ginger and some chopped crystallised ginger (if available) to the mix.

Make icing using lime juice instead of water. Decorate with chopped ginger.

N.B. The above yoghurt recipe works well in the mountains. At home, alter the recipe slightly, e.g. for a small round cake (16 cm) or loaf (20x8cm):

½ pot (60 ml) plain yoghurt & generous ½ pot caster sugar & ½ pot sunflower oil

2 pots plain flour & 2 tsp raising agent

2 eggs

COUNTRY FRUIT LOAF (ALL BRAN CAKE)

This is another chalet host's dream cake. It tastes best after a few days but keeps very well (for up to a month in a cool place!) so it is always worth baking a couple at a time. The clingfilm keeps it lovely and moist, and it is a good nutritious cake, ideal for any health-conscious guests.

1 mug dried fruit and nuts (sultanas, apricots, dates, almonds, walnuts etc)
1 mug milk
1 mug sugar (preferably brown)
1 mug all bran
1 mug plain flour
1 rounded tsp raising agent

Mix all ingredients except flour and raising agent together in a bowl and leave in cool place for at least 4 hours. Add flour and raising agent, mix well and pour into a prepared loaf tin; sprinkle with demerara sugar.
Bake 1 hour at 170C
Remove from tin and wrap immediately in clingfilm.
This is delicious served buttered, like a malt loaf.

FRUIT & NUT BARS

Another fairly healthy (and wheat free!) option for afternoon teas. These bars are also perfect for taking to the slopes for instant energy. They keep well too!

400g condensed milk
250g rolled oats
approx 400g of mixed dried fruit and nuts
e.g., sultanas, shredded coconut, dried cranberries, apricots, mixed seeds (pumpkin, sunflower, sesame), unsalted peanuts, walnuts, almonds

Warm the condensed milk and stir in all other ingredients.
Press into a lined square (20cm) tin.
Bake 45 mins at 120C.
Cut into portions after 15mins and leave to cool completely in tin.

CHOCOLATE KRISPIE CAKES

These are so incredibly easy to make that you will feel almost guilty serving them, but they are always extremely popular with children and adults alike! They also keep well in the fridge so you can make them the day before you need them. Excellent for changeover days.

300g milk chocolate
30g white chocolate
about 10 tbsp rice krispies or cornflakes

Melt milk chocolate, stir in cornflakes/krispies so that each flake is well coated and press well down into a lined square (20cm) tin; drizzle with melted white chocolate.
Cut into squares when nearly set.

BANANA CHOCOLATE BROWNIES

The ultimate indulgence! A tasty way to replace all those calories spent on the slopes (and they must be healthy as they contain bananas!)

If you have children staying these go down well as dessert; warm in the microwave and serve with vanilla ice cream.

200g butter
300g brown sugar
200g dark chocolate, broken into pieces
3 eggs, beaten
2 ripe bananas, mashed
120g plain flour
2 tbsp cocoa powder
1 sachet (11g) raising agent

Mash the bananas roughly and set aside to soften and turn brown.

Put the butter, sugar and chocolate in a pan and heat gently, stirring, until melted and smooth – don't let the mix get too hot.

Re-mash the bananas until they are soft and squidgy and add to mix.

Stir in the beaten eggs and mix well.

Add the flour, cocoa and raising agent and mix well.

Pour into a lined baking tin (about 25x18cm).

Bake for **180C for 30-35 minutes** until firm at edge & softish centre (your test skewer will come out slightly sticky).

Cool in the tin, then turn out and cut into squares, sprinkling with icing sugar if desired.

FLAPJACKS

A perennial favourite, flapjacks are wheat free so bake extra if you have any guests with wheat intolerance.

250g butter
120g runny honey or golden syrup
250g brown sugar (Demerara or soft-brown)
500g porridge oats
pinch of salt

Melt the butter, sugar, salt and syrup/honey slowly in a large saucepan, add oats and mix well, ensuring the oats have absorbed the butter and honey.

Pour into a lined baking tray (about 25 x 18cm) and spread out evenly.

Bake for **15 mins at 190C** until golden brown.

Allow to cool slightly, then melt 50g dark chocolate and drizzle over to decorate.

Cut into portions while still very warm otherwise the knife will "shatter" the flapjacks.

Add a generous handful of raisins or sultanas &/or flaked almonds or coconut to the mix for a nice variation.

COCONUT MACAROONS

1 tin (370ml) sweetened condensed milk
370g desiccated coconut
1 tsp vanilla extract
2 large egg whites, beaten till stiff

Mix the condensed milk, coconut and vanilla in a large bowl.
Carefully fold in the whisked egg whites.
Place tablespoons of the mix onto lined baking trays at least an inch apart.
Bake for about **20 mins at 160C** until golden brown.

FLOURLESS CHOCOLATE BROWNIES

Another wheat free option for afternoon teas.

225g dark choc
225g butter
2 tsp vanilla
200g caster sugar
3 eggs, beaten
150g ground almonds
100g chopped walnuts

Melt choc and butter; add vanilla and sugar and cool slightly.
Beat in eggs; add almonds and walnuts.
Turn into a lined baking tin (about 25x18cm) and bake 25 -30 minutes at 170C.

GINGER SNAPS

This is a useful recipe for cut-out shapes; e.g. stars at Christmas time.
100g plain flour
pinch salt
2 tsp ground ginger
½ tsp raising agent
100g caster sugar
75g butter
2 tbsp golden syrup

Melt butter and syrup, add to dry ingredients, roll out thinly and cut out into shapes.
Bake 10-12 mins at 170 C.
Cool on wire rack.

BANANA BREAD

The bananas and orange juice in this recipe make this a delightfully moist tea bread.

100g sultanas
75ml orange juice
175g plain flour
1 sachet (11g) raising agent
½ tsp salt
125g butter, melted
150g caster sugar
2 eggs (3 if small)
3-4 small, very ripe bananas, mashed with 1 tsp vanilla extract

Place the sultanas and orange juice in a small saucepan and bring to the boil.
Remove from heat, cover and leave for an hour, or until the sultanas have soaked up most of the liquid.
Mix the flour, raising agent and salt together in a bowl.
In a separate bowl, melt the butter, then beat in the sugar followed by the eggs, then the mashed banana.
Stir in the drained sultanas, vanilla extract and then the flour mixture.
Mix well and then scrape into a lined loaf tin.
Bake at **170C for about 1 hour**, until skewer comes out clean.
Leave to cool in the tin, slice and serve.

MOIST CARROT AND GINGER CAKE

This is probably the most popular cake I have ever made!

200 g soft dark brown sugar
150 g plain flour
1 sachet (11g) raising agent
1 tsp ground ginger
130 ml sunflower oil
2 large eggs
250 g carrots, grated
75 g sultanas
75 g stem ginger, chopped

Place sugar, flour, raising agent, ground ginger, oil and eggs in a large bowl & beat well.
Add grated carrot, sultanas and stem ginger, mix well to form a runny batter.
Pour into a loaf tin and bake at **150C until firm - about 50-60 mins**
Cool on wire rack; make basic icing with a good squirt of added lime juice and sprinkle with chopped ginger

DIABETIC FRUIT CAKE

As well as containing no added sugar, this cake has no eggs, so is suitable for anyone with an egg allergy.

450g mixed vine fruits (sultanas/currants/raisins)
2 tbsp brandy or whiskey
225g chopped dates
50g chopped nuts (walnuts or almonds)
2 tsp mixed spice
1 sachet (11g) raising agent
225g plain flour
275ml water
grated rind of 1 lemon and 1 orange

Mix the vine fruits with the brandy or whiskey.
Melt the chopped dates in the warm water gently over low heat or in the microwave & mix with the vine fruits.
Let the mixture stand in a cool place for 3 to 6 hours.
Sift the flour, raising agent and the mixed spice, add the rinds and the chopped nuts.
Combine the flour mixture with the fruit mixture and put in a lined loaf tin.
Bake at **170C for about 50 minutes**.

SHORTBREAD

Very simple and a nice change for those guests who are *caked-out!*

225g butter
100g sugar
250g flour
50g ground almonds (optional)
¼ tsp salt
¼ tsp raising agent

Warm the butter then beat together with the sugar.
Add other ingredients and mix well; you should have a firm ball, if it's to crumbly add a little more butter, if it's too sticky add a bit more flour; then chill in fridge for 10 mins.
Roll out into a rough rectangle about 1cm thick, on a lightly floured surface (you can knead the dough with your hands to achieve this).
Cut into pieces of the desired size and shape, and place on lined baking tray. They will spread during cooking so leave space between each biscuit.
Bake **20-25 minutes at 170C** until golden brown.
Prick with fork to make the traditional patterns and cut any pieces that have *merged* during cooking, then allow to cool.

APERITIFS

Pre-dinner drinks and nibbles are an excellent time to chat with your guests – assuming you've got the dinner under control. Your budget probably won't stretch to G&Ts but don't just serve white wine every night. With a little thought you can offer sparkling drinks to sparkle the conversation.

Strictly speaking, many of these recipes traditionally call for champagne, but cheap (about 1 euro a bottle) sparkling wine makes a good affordable alternative. By itself, the sparkling wine taste fairly disgusting but with mixers it becomes quite palatable. Consider adding a sugar cube to each glass if using dry (*brut*) wine. One bottle will serve 8-12 people when mixed.

Serve sparkling aperitifs in flutes, still drinks in wine goblets or beakers.

In general, it's easier to pour the <u>chilled</u> sparkling wine into a large jug and stir gently to dissipate some bubbles then add any mixer, e.g. cassis, as you stir, then pour into flutes and serve immediately.

KIR ROYALE

Use about 150ml creme de cassis per bottle of fizz.
Variations:
  - Kir Normand: Normandy cider with cassis
  - Kir Breton: Breton cider with cassis

CANALETTO (RASPBERRY FIZZ)

Use tinned raspberries and juice to make ice cubes; place one in each flute and top up with sparkling wine. As the ice melts, long trails of "blood" fill the glass!

CHAMPAGNE COCKTAIL

Place a sugar cube at the bottom of each flute.
Cover with brandy and a couple of drops of angostura bitters, if you have them.
Top up the glasses with sparkling wine.

BUCK'S FIZZ

Mix 300ml orange juice with a bottle of sparkling wine.

MOCK BELLINI

A real Bellini served at Harry's Bar in Venice uses real prosecco and real peaches. This is a cut price cheat's version, but popular none the less.
Liquidize a tin of peaches (about 400g) in the jug then add a bottle of sparkling wine very carefully whilst stirring continuously. It's important to serve immediately as the peach settles.

CALIMOCHO

Mix equal parts of chilled red wine & cola, serve with ice and a slice of orange or lemon. This is a good recipe for getting people talking; ask them to guess the ingredients – you may be very surprised by their answers. In one season, only three people guessed correctly.

VIN CHAUD

1 orange quarter
a dozen or so cloves, stuck into the orange skin (makes it easier to find them later)
2 large cinnamon sticks
1½ litre red wine
50g sugar, half brown (demerara or muscavado) and half white; possibly more to taste
remains of orange and 1 apple, sliced and chopped into small pieces (leave on peel & skin)

Place all ingredients in a large covered pan, bring to the boil, then immediately turn off & leave for at least 30 minutes (but no more than 2 hours else it will taste bitter).
Bring back almost to the boil then taste and possibly add more sugar before serving.
Discard the cloved-orange quarter & the cinnamon sticks before serving.
Ensure each glass has a few pieces of cut fruit in it.

This is a classic drink for cold evenings in front of the log fire.
We often serve this with hot honey-baked sausages and fondue (see Canapes below) out in the snow, often on the guests' last night. In fact we build our own "ice bar" and decorate it with wine bottles and candles.

MULLED WHITE WINE

1 bottle white wine
500ml apple juice
¼ apple, stuck with cloves to taste (I use about 6)
¾ apple, chopped into 1 cm cubes
2 large cinnamon sticks
brown sugar to taste

Heat the wine, apple, apple juice and cinnamon sticks in a saucepan until just boiling.
Remove from the heat and leave for about 30 minutes (do not leave for more than 1 hour as it will become bitter).
Bring back almost to the boil then taste and possibly add sugar before serving.
Remove spices before serving.
This is great on the warmer Spring evenings and few guests have come across it before.

CANAPES

Canapés are pre-dinner nibbles which are served with the aperitifs. The word means *couch* in French, i.e. something sits on top of a pastry/bread base. To save on washing up, it is best if all canapés are finger foods, served with napkins, and cocktail sticks where appropriate. We serve 2 different canapés each night (at least one to suit vegetarians/vegans) and aim to provide 5 or 6 nibbles for each guest.

Don't underestimate the preparation time in your busy evening schedule although many can be prepared in advance.

CUCUMBER CUPS WITH SMOKED SALMON TARTARE

½ large cucumber
100g smoked salmon
10 ml olive oil
juice of 1 lemon
pepper
fresh dill/chives, chopped (or use dried chives with fresh parsley)

Slice the cucumber into 1 cm slices; hollow out one side of the slice using a spoon or knife to form a shallow cup to hold the salmon tartare mix.
Cut the salmon into small pieces and mix with the olive oil, lemon, herbs and seasoning to form the tartare.
Spoon some tartare into each cucumber cup and serve immediately.
Garnish with herbs as desired.

SMOKED SALMON BLINIS

Blinis are a type of pancake, originally from Russia, but also popular in Jewish communities; they can usually be found near the smoked salmon in French supermarkets. For a cheat's version, make small pancakes by using the American pancake recipe (Breakfast section), omitting the sugar.

16 mini blinis
100g cream cheese
100g smoked salmon

Warm the blinis at **180C for 5 minutes**; allow to cool.
Spread with cream cheese and top with strips of smoked salmon.
Garnish with chives if you wish.

HONEY & MUSTARD GLAZED SAUSAGES

550g pack cocktail sausages
125g honey
60g grainy mustard

Put the sausages in a roasting tray lined with baking parchment with a little oil.
Bake for **20 mins at 180C** (turn once).
Mix the honey with the mustard, pour over the sausages and cook for a further **20mins** (turning once) until the sausages are nicely sticky.
These look particularly impressive served in a hollowed out loaf and are a good complement to vin chaud aperitif.

CREAM CHEESE AND PEPPER WRAPS

3 soft tortilla wraps
75g cream cheese
1 red pepper (if you like you can roast & remove skin), cut into thin strips
10g fresh mint, chopped (or 1 tsp dried mint)

Spread 1/3 of the cheese over each tortilla followed by strips of pepper; sprinkle with mint.
Roll up the tortilla as tightly as possible, then wrap tightly in cling film.
Refrigerate for at least 4 hours.
Remove the cling film and cut off the untidy ends.
Cut each tortilla roll into 3 equal pieces, then cut each of those pieces into 2 at an angle.
Serve immediately.

CHEESE AND OLIVE SCONES

2 onions, diced
12 pitted black olives, chopped
100g parmesan, grated
50g emmental, grated
350g plain flour
4 tsp raising agent
1 tsp salt
1 tsp mustard powder
1 tsp cayenne pepper
50g butter
2 eggs, beaten
4-5 tbsp milk

Fry the onion until lightly browned.
Mix dry ingredients (flour & seasonings) together; rub in butter; mix in onion, about 2/3 of the cheeses and the olives.
Add eggs and enough milk to form a soft dough.
Roll out to about 2 cm thick and cut out with a floured egg cup.
Brush scones with milk or beaten egg, sprinkle with remaining cheese and bake **10-12 minutes at 200C** until golden**.**

BLUE CHEESE AND WALNUT CROSTINI

200g blue cheese
50g chopped walnuts
16 slices toasted French stick
Mix cheese and walnuts, spread on toasts, bake **5 minutes at 200 C** or grill until bubbling.

GOATS CHEESE CROSTINIS

Slice a part baked baguette into 1 cm thick slices.
Bake **5 mins at 190C.**
Top with slices of goats cheese; bake for another **5 mins.**

PISSALADIERE

1 ready-made pizza base
1 small jar pizza topping (or tomato puree with mixed herbs)
1 small tin anchovies

Spread base with pizza topping.
Arrange anchovies in criss-cross pattern.
Bake **10-15 mins at 200C.**
Cut into squares.

SPICY SMASHED CHICKPEAS

410g can chickpeas, drained
100 ml tahini paste
1 tsp harissa paste
100g sun-dried tomatoes in oil (optional)
2 cloves garlic, crushed
2 tbsp lemon juice
2 tbsp olive oil
salt and pepper, to taste

This is similar to hummous. Tahini paste is made from sesame seeds and gives an authentic flavour ; if you can't get it, try replacing it with a tablespoon of sesame oil, or olive oil with a handful of sesame seeds. As an alternative to harissa, use a little chilli powder or crushed dried chillies for a bit of a kick.
Blend all ingredients, taste and add extra oil or lemon juice as required; drizzle with olive oil and sprinkle with paprika to serve.
Serve with celery and carrot batons, tortilla chips or strips of pitta bread.
Tips: *for a smoother textured hummous, tip chickpeas into a saucepan, cover with fresh water and heat through before blending.*
For a change, replace the tahini & tomatoes with a jar of flame-roasted red peppers in oil, or some apricots.

MARINATED OLIVES

Mix 1 jar of olives (green or black, or a mixture) with a good sprinkling of oregano, a ripped up bay leaf and 1-2 crumbled dried chillies.
Season with black pepper, fennel seeds or cracked coriander seeds.
Cover with olive oil and <u>keep</u> in an airtight container for at least 2 hours before serving.
These will keep for several days in the fridge.

PESTO WHIRLS

1 sheet puff pastry
1 small jar pesto (red or green)

Cut a rectangle of pastry about 20cm square; spread with pesto and roll up tightly from 2 opposite sides.
Wrap in clingfilm and chill for a couple of hours.
Slice ½ cm thick and lay on baking tray.
Bake about **10 minutes at 200-220 C.**

CHEESE STRAWS

This one is good for using up leftover pastry scraps and pieces of cheese.
Mix pastry trimmings with as much grated mixed cheeses as you can incorporate (e.g. parmesan and emmental).
Roll out about 1cm thick and cut into strips about 1cm wide, 5-10cm long.
Put a few twists into each strip, lay on baking tray and sprinkle with extra cheese.
Bake about **10 mins at 200-220 C.**
Serve hot or cold.

DEVILS AND ANGELS

Another amazing complement to vin chaud!
1 pack bacon rashers
~12 apricots
~12 dates or prunes

Cut each bacon slice into 2 pieces and wrap each piece around a stoned date, prune or apricot.
Bake about **20 minutes at 180C.**

STUFFED MUSHROOMS

16 button mushrooms
~200g boursin (cream cheese with herbs and garlic)
~50g gruyere cheese

Remove stalks from the mushrooms, stuff with boursin and top with a small slice of gruyere.
Bake for about **15 minutes at 180C.**

CHEESE DISCS

100g g cheese (any type, or a mix but not too much soft or blue)
100g g butter
120g plain flour
seasoning (e.g. cumin, oregano, black pepper, caraway seeds)
coating (e.g. crushed peppercorns, mixed herbs or sesame seeds)

Mix in food processor the cheese, butter, seasoning and flour to smooth dough.
Divide in 3 and form into a sausage shape.
Roll in your chosen coating, wrap in clingfilm or foil and **chill for several hours.**
Slice into discs and **bake 7-10 minutes at 200C** until golden.

FROGS' LEGS

One of the easiest canapés; when in France, do as the French do!
Always have a safe alternative to this one as many guests are squeamish and won't try them; they're expensive so reserve them for your favourite guests!
16 frogs' legs (defrosted)
30ml sunflower oil
salt and pepper

Put all the ingredients in a plastic bag and shake until the legs are coated with oil.
Lay out on a baking sheet; cook at **200C for 10-15 minutes** until golden.

SNAILS IN GARLIC BUTTER

You don't have to stuff the snails yourself! They come ready prepared, for another dead easy canapé but heed the advice above for frogs.

1 pack of frozen snails in garlic butter (we defrost for a couple of hours first, but I don't think it's strictly necessary)

Place the snails on a baking tray, trying to position them so that the butter doesn't all run out as it melts. Cook at **180C for 15 minutes**, until the butter has melted, releasing a lovely garlicky aroma. Serve with cocktail sticks for hooking the snails out of their shells.

TOMATO BRUSCHETTAS

8 slices French stick
4 tbsp olive oil
4 tomatoes, diced
2 handfuls chopped basil

Brush the bread slices with half the olive oil; bake for about 10 mins at 200C until golden.
Mix the tomatoes, basil and remaining olive oil in a bowl.
Spoon tomato mixture on top of the toasts.

SAUCES & DRESSINGS

These sauces/dressings may be used with several dishes and are tastier than many shop-bought ones. The quantities given make enough for one meal (8 people) but you can make bigger batches and keep in the fridge.

VINAIGRETTE SALAD DRESSING

½ garlic clove, crushed
pinch salt
1- 2 tbsp lemon juice (or wine/balsamic vinegar)
6 tbsp olive oil
pepper

Crush garlic with salt to a paste; add lemon juice and then oil; season with pepper and mix well.

BALSAMIC VINEGAR DRESSING

Mix one part of balsamic vinegar with 3 parts of olive oil and a good grinding of pepper, in a screw top jar. Shake well before use.

BALSAMIC JUS

Best to make this when the guests are out as it pongs a bit!
200ml balsamic vinegar
100g sugar
Simmer together for about 15 minutes until the volume is reduced by about half.
You will need to experiment a little as the exact amount of ingredients will depend on the type of sugar and vinegar used.
Tip: *put in fridge prior to use to thicken it slightly.*

SWEET CHILLI SAUCE

½ cup vinegar
½ cup vegetable stock
2 cloves garlic, finely chopped
1 cup sugar
2 tbsp fresh ginger, grated (optional)
2 fresh red chilli, finely chopped (or 1 tsp dried crumbled chillies)
Heat the vinegar and stock fiercely on the stove then add the sugar.
Add the garlic, ginger and chilli.
Allow to reduce for **20 mins** on a gentle heat.
Taste and season as required.

MARIE ROSE SAUCE

3 tbsp ketchup
3 tbsp mayonnaise
1 tbsp Worcester sauce
1 tbsp lemon juice
Place all the dressing ingredients in a bowl or jar; mix well and cool in fridge.

MUSTARD MAYONNAISE DRESSING

2 tbsp mayonnaise

2 tbsp wine vinegar

6 tbsp sunflower oil

2 tsp Dijon mustard

2 tsp dried tarragon

Put the mayonnaise, mustard, vinegar and tarragon into a bowl and add the oil while stirring all the time.

STARTERS

SALAD SAVOYARDE

1 batavia lettuce, washed and drained well (this type has crisp "frilly" leaves without a hard heart with a nutty flavour; other types can be substituted)
2 good handfuls of mache (lambs tongue lettuce)
100g bread, cubed or torn into croutons
250g lardons
250g emmental cheese, cubed
4 hard-boiled eggs (or 8 poached eggs if you prefer – personally I don't! They may be more authentic, but it's tricky getting 8 poached eggs ready at the same time.)
mustard mayonnaise dressing (see separate recipe).

Place the lardons on a baking tray and bake at **180C for about 10 minutes**.
Pour off excess juices, stir in the bread cubes and bake for **another 5 – 10 minutes** until crispy; set aside and reheat just before serving.
Rip the lettuce up, add washed mache, and toss in the dressing.
Divide the dressed salad between the plates, top with cheese, croutons and lardons; serve immediately.

CHICKPEA AND GINGER SALAD

2 tsp cumin seeds
800g tin chickpeas, drained and rinsed
3 peppers (red, orange or yellow)
2 red onions, diced
4 cm piece root ginger, grated or finely chopped
about 50ml lemon juice
30g sugar (optional, to taste)
salt and pepper
handful of chopped coriander, to serve

Fry the cumin in a hot, dry pan until lightly toasted and fragrant.
Mix all ingredients together, season to taste and serve garnished with coriander.
Strips of warm pitta bread are a good accompaniment.

ROASTED TOMATO, MOZZARELLA AND PESTO SALAD

1 large pack of rocket or mixed salad leaves
~40 cherry tomatoes
1 or 2 red peppers (optional), roughly cut
2 balls mozzarella, cut into 1cm slices
handful basil leaves, torn up
¼ small jar pesto
3 tbsp olive oil
50g pine nuts, dry fried until lightly toasted

Put tomatoes (and peppers if used) into baking dish, brush with olive oil and season.
Bake for about **10 minutes at 200C** until tomatoes split.
Add mozzarella and bake for a further minute or two until the cheese starts to ooze.
Arrange the salad leaves on plate, top with tomatoes and oozing mozzarella, scatter with basil leaves.
Mix pesto and olive oil to make dressing, drizzle generously over the salad and scatter with toasted pine nuts.

ROCKET, PEAR AND PARMESAN SALAD

4 ripe pears, peeled and cut up in chunks
200g rocket, washed
100g walnuts, crumbled
50g block parmesan, shaved with a vegetable peeler
olive oil
lemon juice (preferably freshly squeezed)

Mix the pear and rocket together, drizzle with olive oil and a squeeze of lemon juice.
Top with walnuts and parmesan shavings.

PRAWN COCKTAIL

400g frozen prawns, defrosted and drained
1 large lettuce
2 lemons, cut into quarters
Marie Rose Sauce (see separate recipe)

Prepare a Marie Rose sauce and cool in fridge for at least an hour, before mixing with the prawns.
Arrange lettuce on a plate, top with prawns and a piece of lemon.

SALMON MOUSSE

250g smoked salmon (off-cut pieces are fine)
250g cream cheese
2 tbsp lemon juice
pepper

Blitz the ingredients into a fine puree.
Serve with lambs lettuce, a lemon segment and crackers (or small toasts) with a sprinkle of chopped dill.

APPLE & REBLOCHON (OR BRIE) BRUSCHETTA

75g butter
75g brown sugar
3 apples, peeled, cored and cut into eight pieces
8 slices French bread, cut on a long diagonal in 1 cm slices, toasted or baked until light golden
small reblochon (or brie) cheese, sliced
salad garnish
balsamic *jus* dressing (see separate recipe)

Place the butter and sugar in a saucepan and cook until melted.
Add the apples and cook for five to ten minutes, until caramelised and cooked through.
Lay out the toasts on a large baking tray, cover with the apple (with all the lovely juices) and then the cheese slices, grill or roast at **180C for 5-10 mins**, until melted.
Garnish with a green salad with walnuts and a balsamic *jus* dressing .

MARGHERITA SALAD

mixed salad leaves (e.g.1 pack mache and 1 pack rocket)
2 balls mozzarella, sliced about 1 cm thick (marinated for 2 hours)
large handful basil leaves, chopped
handful chopped parsley
6tbsp olive oil
black pepper

For the crispy crumb dressing:
4 large tomatoes
about 20 basil leaves
150g breadcrumbs
100g grated parmesan
2 tbsp olive oil

Mix the herbs, oil and pepper; pour over cheese slices in a shallow dish, cover and marinate in the fridge for 2-3 hours.
Cut the tomatoes in half; remove the seeds; dice the flesh; mix with basil.
Roast tomatoes at **200C for 10 mins.**
Add crumbs, parmesan, and oil; roast for further **10 mins.**
Arrange salad leaves on plate, top with mozzarella; scatter with crumbs.

CRISPY DUCK SALAD WITH SPICY PLUM SAUCE

Readily available in French supermarkets (but not British!), *Confit de canard* is duck which has been tinned and pre-cooked in its own fat.

4 portions Confit de Canard
1 pack rocket
1 pack mache   (lambs lettuce)
1 large carrot, peeled
1 pack radishes, washed, topped and tailed and thinly sliced
(or any mix of salad ingredients, e.g. Batavia lettuce with watercress and strips of red pepper).

100ml sweet chilli sauce (see separate recipe)
½ jar plum (or cherry) jam

See the recipe for Confit de Canard in the Main Courses section for details of how to extract duck pieces from the tin.
Reheat the duck pieces in a baking tray in the oven at **150C for about 30 mins**, as it makes shredding it easier.
Discard as much fat as possible.
Remove the duck skin and use a pair of forks to pull apart, or shred, the duck meat.
Ensure you find all 3 bones in the leg, 1 may be quite small.
Spread out the shreds in the tin and roast for about **15 mins at 200C** until crispy, turning occasionally.

Meanwhile heat the plum jam and chilli sauce in a small saucepan to combine.
Arrange the salad ingredients on plates, using a potato peeler to form decorative strips of carrot.
 Top with the crispy duck and drizzle with sauce.

CARAMELISED RED ONION TARTS

2 packs ready rolled puff pastry
25g butter
2 large red onions, thinly sliced
4 garlic cloves, peeled & thinly sliced
1 tsp dried thyme
1 tbsp caster sugar
salt and pepper
200g creme fraiche
balsamic *jus* dressing (see separate recipe)

Melt the butter in a large pan. Add the onions, garlic and thyme and cook gently for about **20 minutes**, until deep brown and caramelised. Season to taste with salt and pepper, add the sugar then cook for another few minutes.
Tip: cook a big batch of onions and freeze in portions for subsequent weeks.

Cut out pastry circles & put in individual patty tins.
Using a fork, pierce the pastry bases a few times and then place in the oven to **blind bake (220C) for 5 mins;** press pastry down with a fork; bake for a further 5 mins.
Remove the cooked pastry bases from the oven (this can be done well before serving).

Drop creme fraiche into each pastry base, top with the caramelised onions,
and return to the oven for a few minutes immediately prior to serving.

Serve with rocket or mache and an artistic swirl of balsamic jus.

Other fillings can be used for a variety of tarts, e.g.:
     -a slice of goats cheese drizzled with honey, topped with half a walnut
     -half a tomato drizzled with olive oil and sprinkled with dried basil

PENNE ALLE SALMONE

500g penne pasta
200g smoked salmon trimmings
300g cream cheese
lemon juice
black pepper
chopped parsley or chives

Cook the pasta in boiling salted water until al dente (about 10 minutes).
Drain, keeping a cupful of the liquid.
Stir in the cream cheese and salmon, and add enough of the cooking liquid to make a smooth sauce.
Season with lemon juice and black pepper.
Serve sprinkled with chopped fresh herbs.

CHEESE RISOTTO (AND MUSHROOM RISOTTO)

This is a basic risotto recipe which you can adjust as you like. I like it best made with cheddar cheese, but gruyere or parmesan are good (and probably more authentic) alternatives. You can replace the cheese with mushrooms and crushed garlic for mushroom risotto.

30ml olive oil
2 leeks or onions, finely chopped
450g risotto rice, rinsed
150ml white wine
approx 1.2 litre hot vegetable stock
150g grated cheddar, gruyere or parmesan

Heat the olive oil, and cook the vegetables gently until softened.
Add the rice and stir to fry the rice without letting it colour at all; keep it moving all the time, and after 2-3 minutes it will begin to look translucent.
Add the wine, still stirring all the time.
Once the wine seems to have cooked into the rice, add a ladle of hot stock and a pinch of salt. Turn down the heat to a simmer.
Keep adding ladlefuls of stock, stirring and allowing each ladleful to be fully absorbed before adding the next. This will take about **15 mins**. Carry on adding stock until the rice is soft but with a slight bite.
Add the cheese and check seasoning.
Sprinkle with chopped chives or parsley and serve immediately.

THAI FISHCAKES WITH SWEET CHILLI SAUCE

500g white fish
1 fresh red chilli, finely chopped
2 cloves garlic, crushed
juice & rind of a lime
2 large potatoes
handful coriander leaves, chopped
1 tsp fresh ginger, grated
1 tsp soy sauce
handful breadcrumbs or flour (if required)
salt and pepper
salad for garnishing
sweet chilli sauce (see separate recipe).

Boil the potatoes until soft; mash well.
Place the fish in a large pan, cover with cold water and bring to the boil; poach for **5-10 mins** until it flakes apart; remove any skin.
Put the coriander, ginger and garlic in a mixing bowl; flake the fish into this, then add all other ingredients, mix together and season to taste.
If the mixture is too soft or runny to hold together, add some breadcrumbs or flour until it will hold in a ball.
Divide the mixture into 8 large patties (or 16 smaller ones), then pan fry until golden brown on both sides; finish in a hot oven for 10-15 minutes until firm.
Serve with a salad garnish and sweet chilli sauce.

BAKED CAMEMBERT WITH CRUSTY BREAD

3 rounds camembert
3 cloves garlic, peeled and sliced
dried thyme
olive oil
1 large baguette /flute

This is really an easy sort of fondue!
Remove the camemberts from the boxes, take off the paper and replace with foil; put back in the box (throw the lid away).
Insert the garlic into the cheese, sprinkle with a little dried thyme and olive oil; fold the foil over to enclose the cheese; bake for about **20 mins at 180C.**
Cut the bread into chunky sticks and bake for about 10 mins till light golden brown (this makes the bread much easier to dip into the melted cheese).

To serve, remove excess foil and place the boxes on the dining table (then be prepared to clean up the mess!)

CHEESE FONDUE

We often serve a fondue with hot aperitifs at our ice bar, outside in the snow, but it can also be served as a starter at the table. You need a fondue pot, which is kept warm with a little oil burner or candles, and long handled fondue forks for dipping the bread etc.

700g chopped or grated cheese (any mix of emmental, brie, camembert, gruyere etc....)
300ml white wine
2 tsp cornflour
2 tbsp kirsh (optional)
2 cloves garlic, peeled
good grinding of pepper and nutmeg

to serve: carrot sticks, pepper, chicory, bread etc......

Put cheese and wine in fondue pot and heat on hob till boiling.
Slake the cornflour with kirsh or water and add to the pot with the garlic.
Continue heating for a few minutes until smooth.
Season with pepper and serve.

ARTICHOKE HEART & PARMESAN GRATINS

25g butter
2 onions, roughly chopped
100g lardons (omit for vegetarians)
230g tin artichoke hearts, drained and chopped
100ml cream
75g grated parmesan
75g grated emmental
1 egg yolk
pepper

Melt the butter and fry the onions gently for about 10 mins until soft, in a medium-sized saucepan.
Add the lardons and cook for five minutes.
Take the pan off the heat.
Add the artichoke, 1/2 of the cheese, egg yolk and seasoning and mix roughly,
then add the cream and mix well (this avoids curdling).
Spoon into greased ramekins & sprinkle with the remaining cheese.
Clean the tops of the ramekins and bake at **200C for 15 - 20 minutes** until golden brown on top.

SEAFOOD GRATINS

4 tbsp olive oil
3 large onions, peeled & chopped
3 garlic cloves, crushed
4 tbsp chopped parsley
800g can chopped tomatoes
pinch sugar
2 tbsp tomato puree
150g feta cheese
Seafood: either 250g prawns or 2 tins (185g each) tuna, drained; or a mixture of both

Saute the onions in oil for 5 minutes, add garlic, herbs, sugar, tomatoes and puree.
Simmer **30 mins** until thickened.
Stir in prawns &/or tuna.
Pour into greased ramekins; crumble feta over; bake **5 -10mins at 200C.**
Serve in ramekins on a saucer and warn your guests they're HOT!

FISH FINGER GRATINS

70g butter
70g flour
750ml milk
handful of finely-chopped fresh parsley (or 1 tsp dried parsley)
150g grated cheese (either gruyere or a mix of emmental and parmesan)
8 fish fingers

Grill or fry the fish fingers for about 5 mins each side.
Meanwhile, melt the butter in a small pan, stir in the flour and cook for 1-2 mins to make a roux; slowly add the milk, a little at a time, cooking to thicken after each addition; add the parsley and season to taste.
Chop the cooked fish fingers into chunks; stir into the sauce.
Pour into greased ramekins, sprinkle with cheese and bake for **10 mins at 200C,** or grill till cheese bubbles.
For **MUSHROOM GRATINS**, replace fish fingers with 250g lightly fried mushrooms.

SOUPE DU JOUR

The French restaurants invariably serve this – *soup of the day* - which is basically a soup made from whatever they happen to have in stock! It's usually vegetable based and can be made by adapting one of the above recipes, e.g. leek and potato. Whenever we have left over vegetables from dinner-time, e.g. potatoes, carrots, cauliflower, leeks (but generally not peas and beans) we freeze them and later use them for soup. Simply sweat a couple of onions (or use 2-3 tbsp onion base), add stock and vegetables and simmer until the vegetables are soft. Blend and season to taste. Serve with croutons and grated cheese.

SOUPE DU SAVOYARDE

This is unique to the Savoie region of the Alps and is made from leftovers of their local dish, *tartiflette*, which is a potato, bacon and cheese dish. Freeze leftover tartiflette having first discarded the baked cheese crust. When required, simply defrost and add broccoli (frozen is fine) and stock; boil for 10 mins then blend until smooth.

FRENCH ONION SOUP

700g onions, thinly sliced
3 tbsp olive oil
70 g butter
3 cloves garlic, crushed
1 level tsp granulated sugar
1500ml beef stock
300ml white wine
salt and freshly milled black pepper

On a high heat, melt the oil and butter together. When this is very hot, add the onions, garlic and sugar, and keep turning them from time to time until the edges of the onions have turned dark – this will take about 5 minutes. Then reduce the heat to its lowest setting and leave the onions to carry on **cooking very slowly for about 30 minutes**, by which time the base of the pan will be covered with a rich, nut brown, caramelised film. After that, pour in the stock and white wine, season, and then stir with a wooden spoon, scraping the base of the pan well. As soon as it all comes up to simmering point, turn down the heat to its lowest setting, then leave it to cook very gently, without a lid, for **about 1 hour**.
For extra warming effect, add a couple of tablespoons of Cognac before serving (if your chalet budget can afford it!).

Croutons:
French bread, cut into 1 inch (2.5 cm) diagonal slices
2 tbsp olive oil
2 cloves garlic, crushed
400g Gruyère, grated
Mix the oil and crushed garlic together. Dip each slice of bread in the oil so that both sides are lightly coated.
Bake at 180C for about 15 mins till golden.
Now sprinkle the grated cheese thickly over the croutons and place in the oven until the cheese is golden brown and bubbling.
Ladle the soup into warm bowls, float a crouton on top and serve immediately.

LEEK AND POTATO SOUP

750g leeks
3 large potatoes, peeled and cut into chunks
2 onions, chopped
1.5 litres hot chicken or vegetable stock
350ml milk
70g butter
salt and pepper
crème fraiche and chopped chives/parsley to serve

Trim the leeks, discarding the tough outer layer. Split them in half lengthways and slice them quite finely, then wash them thoroughly in two or three changes of water. Drain well.
In a large, thick-based saucepan, gently melt the butter, then add the leeks, onions and potatoes, stirring them all round with a wooden spoon so they get a good coating of butter. Season with salt and pepper, then cover and let the vegetables sweat over a very low heat for about **15 mins**.
Add the stock and milk, bring to simmering point, cover and let the soup simmer very gently for a further **20 mins** or until the vegetables are soft – if you have the heat too high the milk in it may cause it to boil over.
Blend and taste to check the seasoning. Add a swirl of cream or crème fraîche before serving and sprinkle with freshly snipped chives or parsley.

TUSCAN BEAN SOUP

2 x 400g cans mixed beans, drained and rinsed
4 tbsp sunflower oil
2 medium onions, finely chopped
2 cloves garlic, crushed or finely chopped
2 carrots, peeled and diced
2 sticks celery, chopped
2 x400g cans chopped tomatoes
2 tbsp tomato puree
1200ml vegetable stock
4 sprigs fresh thyme or 1tsp dried thyme
2 bay leaves
salt and freshly ground black pepper

Heat the oil in a large saucepan and fry the onion gently for about **5 mins** until soft.
Stir in the garlic, carrot, celery and continue to cook for a further **5 mins**.
Add the tomatoes, tomato puree, stock, herbs and seasoning.
Bring to the boil, then reduce the heat to a simmer, cover and cook, stirring occasionally, for about **30 mins** or until the vegetables are soft.
Remove half of the vegetable mixture and blend the rest until smooth, then add the unblended vegetables back to the pan.
Add the beans, and simmer for a further **10 mins** or until the beans have been heated through. Check seasoning and serve with a sprig of basil or a swirl of pesto.

QUICK TOMATO SOUP

1 onion, peeled and finely chopped
2 carrots, chopped
2 medium potatoes, peeled and chopped
2 red peppers, chopped
800g tinned tomatoes
2 veg stock cubes made up to 2 litres with boiling water
2 tbsp tomato puree
salt and pepper.

Place all ingredients in a large pan, bring to the boil and simmer for **30 mins** or until the vegetables are tender. Blend and season, adding Worcestershire sauce to taste, if desired. Serve with a swirl of cream.

RED LENTIL SOUP

800g tinned tomatoes
150g red lentils
200g onions, peeled and finely chopped
2 veg stock cubes made up to 1.5 litres with boiling water
2 tsp ground cumin
1 large clove of garlic, crushed
1 tbsp brown sugar
1 tbsp Worcestershire sauce
1 tbsp tomato puree
 salt and pepper.

Sweat the onion in a little sunflower oil for **5 – 10 mins** until soft.
Add the garlic and tomatoes and cook for a couple of minutes.
Add the rest of the ingredients except the salt (it toughens the lentils).
Cover and simmer for **30 mins** or until the lentils are tender.
Blend and season.
Serve with a dollop of cream or crème fraiche topped with a sprinkle of herbs.

CARROT AND CORIANDER SOUP

2 tbsp sunflower oil
2 onions, sliced
1kg carrots, sliced
2 tsp ground coriander
2 litres vegetable stock
large bunch fresh coriander, roughly chopped
salt and freshly ground black pepper

Heat the oil in a large pan and add the onions and the carrots; cook for a few minutes until the vegetables soften slightly, stir in the ground coriander and season well. Cook for 1 minute. Add the vegetable stock and bring to the boil.
Simmer until the vegetables are tender (this may take up to an hour).
Add half the fresh coriander and blend until smooth. Stir in the remaining coriander .

MAIN COURSES

CHICKEN RECIPES

See also Savoyarde chicken in the Savoyarde specialities section later. And some turkey recipes will suit chicken too.

CHICKEN IN CHEESE AND CIDER SAUCE

8 chicken breasts (can also use legs/thighs)
30ml olive oil
2 onions, chopped
30g plain flour
500ml cider
pinch mixed herbs
salt and pepper
2 tsp Dijon mustard
100g strong cheddar or gruyere cheese
150ml single cream

Fry the chicken in the oil until lightly browned, add the onion and cook till soft.
Stir in flour and cook for 1-2 minutes, then add cider slowly until chicken is covered.
Bring to the boil, add herbs and seasoning and **simmer for 30 minutes**.
Add cream, mustard and half the cheese without boiling.
Transfer to an ovenproof dish, sprinkle with the rest of the cheese and brown under the grill or in a hot oven.

COQ AU VIN

This is the quintessential French chicken casserole; it doesn't mind hanging around for a while if your guests are late, so it is a good one for changeover days..

8 chicken legs, sprinkled with a little flour
30g butter
1 tbsp olive oil
4 garlic cloves, chopped
16 small shallots, peeled
250g whole button mushrooms
good pinch of dried thyme
500ml red wine
500ml chicken stock
2 tbsp chopped fresh parsley
salt and freshly ground black pepper

Heat the butter with the oil in a large pan, add the garlic and shallots and sauté for about 5 minutes until softened.
Remove from the pan and set aside while you brown the chicken legs a few at a time in the pan.
Put the shallots and garlic back in the pan with the mushrooms and thyme and sauté for 5 minutes.
Pour in the wine and stock and bring to the boil.
Reduce the heat and **simmer for about 60 minutes** until the chicken is thoroughly cooked through.
Remove the chicken pieces to a warmed serving dish with a slotted spoon.
Increase the heat and boil the sauce until reduced by about half (or thicken with cornflour). Pour the sauce over the chicken pieces and sprinkle with parsley before serving.

CHICKEN BASQUE

This is a complete meal in a pot; saves on washing up but you do need a very large pot!

8 chicken quarters, seasoned with salt and pepper
4 large red peppers, sliced
3 onions, sliced
100g sun-dried tomatoes in oil, cut into 1 cm pieces
3 tbsp extra virgin olive oil
3 large cloves garlic, chopped
200g chorizo sausage, skinned and cut into 1 cm slices
brown basmati rice measured to the 400 ml level in a glass measuring jug
500ml chicken stock
300 ml white wine
2 tbsp tomato purée
1 tsp hot paprika
2 tsp mixed fresh herbs
100g pitted black olives
2 oranges, peeled and cut into wedges
salt and pepper

Brown the chicken in oil in a large pot.
Remove chicken from pot, add the onion and peppers and fry for about 5 minutes.
Add the garlic, chorizo and dried tomatoes and stir for a minute or two until the garlic is pale golden and the chorizo has taken on some colour.
Next, stir in the rice and, when the grains are coated with oil, add the stock, wine, tomato purée and paprika. Bring to the boil and then turn the heat down to a gentle simmer.
Add a little more seasoning, then place the chicken gently on top of everything, making sure to keep the rice down in the liquid.
Finally, sprinkle the herbs over the chicken pieces and scatter the olives and wedges of orange in among them.
Cover with a tight-fitting lid and **simmer gently for 50-60 minutes** until the rice is cooked but still retains a little bite.
Alternatively cook in a pre-heated oven 180°C for 1 hour.

SLOW-ROASTED CHICKEN

8 chicken portions with skin on
2 heads garlic, separated into unpeeled cloves
large handful fresh thyme (pull leaves roughly off stalks)
4 tbsp olive oil
100 ml white wine
black pepper

Put the chicken, garlic, oil and thyme in a large roasting tin.
Use your hands to mix it all up and then spread out chicken pieces, skin side up.
Pour on the wine, grind on some pepper, then cover tightly with foil and put in oven for **2 hours at 160C.**
Remove foil, pour off excess liquid, turn up oven and roast for a **further 30-45 mins at 200C.**

HUNTER'S CHICKEN (CHICKEN CHASSEUR)

2 tbsp olive oil
2 cloves garlic, peeled and crushed
200g lardons
1 large onion, finely chopped
1 tsp rosemary, finely chopped
1 kg boneless chicken meat, diced (leg or thigh meat has more flavour)
1 tbsp plain flour
250ml white wine
2 x 400g cans chopped tomatoes
3 bay leaves
½ tsp sugar

Put the oil into a large pan with the lardons, garlic, onions and rosemary and fry for a couple of minutes.
Add the bite-sized chicken pieces, stirring well, and season with salt and pepper; stir in flour and cook for a couple of minutes.
Pour in the wine and let it come to a bubble before adding the tomatoes, bay leaves and sugar. Put the lid on and let the pan **simmer for 20-30 minutes**, until the chicken is cooked through.
Thicken if necessary by reduction or with a little slaked cornflour.

CHICKEN PROVENCAL

8 chicken breasts
16 slices of smoked steaky bacon
4 tbsp dark soy sauce
2 tbsp Worcestershire sauce
2 tbsp runny honey
2 tbsp olive oil
2 tbsp lemon juice
1 tbsp dried sage, or about 8 fresh leaves
1 tbsp grainy mustard
1 chicken stock cube
800g tinned tomatoes
2 tbsp tomato puree
50g black olives, stoned
salt and pepper
2 tbsp crème fraiche and fresh chopped parsley to serve

Wrap bacon around each chicken breast and place into a greased ovenproof dish, leaving a space around each piece.
Combine all the ingredients for the sauce, blend with a hand blender and pour over the chicken.
Bake uncovered in oven at **180C for 45 minutes,** basting every 15 minutes.
When cooked, pour off the sauce and stir crème fraiche into it and season to taste.
Slice the breasts diagonally to serve, spoon sauce over and sprinkle with chopped parsley.

CHICKEN MONTAGNARDE

8 chicken breast fillets
200g garlic and herb soft cheese (e.g. Boursin or cheaper own brand)
16 slices of smoked bacon (or can use parma ham or pancetta)
200ml white wine
200ml hot water
1 chicken stock cube
2 cloves garlic, peeled and crushed
2 tsp cornflour mixed with 2 tbsp cold water
300ml cream
small knob of butter
salt and pepper
fresh chopped parsley to serve

Cut a pocket in the side of the chicken breast and push some of the cheese into the space.
Wrap bacon around each chicken piece and place into a greased ovenproof dish.
Heat the wine, water, stock cube, garlic, salt and pepper in a saucepan and when boiling pour over the chicken.
Cover with foil and bake in oven at **180C for 40 minutes.**
After this time pour the liquid into a saucepan and return the chicken to the oven, uncovered, for a further 10 minutes to crisp up the bacon.
Use about 300ml of cooking liquid to make the sauce; add slaked cornflour to thicken.
Add the cream and season as required.
Just before serving add the knob of butter.

THAI CURRY (RED OR GREEN)

2 tbsp sunflower oil
small bunch spring onions

2 green peppers, deseeded and cut into strips
4 tbsp thai green curry paste
OR use red peppers and red paste

1 kg chicken meat, cut into thin strips
400ml can coconut milk
250ml chicken stock (optional)
1 tbsp fish sauce (optional)
400g frozen green beans
lime wedges and chopped coriander to serve

Heat oil in a large pan and fry spring onions and pepper for a couple of minutes.
Stir in curry paste followed by chicken; fry gently for another few minutes.
Add coconut milk.
Add fish sauce if desired, and stock if needed to thin down the sauce.
Simmer for 10 minutes.
Add beans and simmer for another 5 minutes.
Serve with rice or noodles, chopped coriander and lime wedges.

MOROCCAN CHICKEN

1 kg chicken breast,
2 tbsp sunflower oil
1 large onion, finely chopped
2 cloves garlic (or 2 tsp garlic powder)
½ tsp cinnamon
2 tsp cumin
2 tsp ground ginger
2 tsp paprika
1 tbsp harissa paste or ½ tsp chilli powder
8 dried apricots, chopped
8 prunes, chopped
About 500ml apple juice
1 bay leaf
400g tin chopped tomatoes
400g tin chickpeas, drained and rinsed

Put the oil into a large pan with onions and sweat until soft. Add spices and garlic and cook for about a minute. Add the bite-sized chicken pieces, stirring well, and season with salt and pepper before adding the apricots, prunes, tomatoes, bay leaves and apple juice to cover. Put the lid on and **simmer for 20-30 minutes**, until the chicken is cooked through.
Add the chickpeas and heat through.
Serve with couscous and roasted Mediterranean vegetables.

TURKEY RECIPES

Some chicken recipes will suit turkey too.

TURKEY STROGANOFF

4 tbsp olive oil
3 onions, cut into thin half moons
450g mushrooms, sliced
8 turkey fillets, cut into strips
100g plain flour
1 tbsp paprika
400ml white wine
1 tbsp Dijon mustard
dash of Worcester sauce
200ml crème fraiche or double cream
1 lemon, cut into wedges, to serve

Heat 1 tbsp of the olive oil in a pan and add onions; sweat gently on low heat with the pan covered until softened (about 10 minutes).
Heat the rest of the olive oil in a frying pan, roll the turkey strips in plain flour, paprika, salt and pepper and fry for 3-4 minutes until browned (in batches if necessary).
Add the white wine, Dijon mustard, Worcester sauce and chopped mushrooms to the pan with the onions in them and cook for 3 minutes.
Add the cooked turkey and simmer for about 15 minutes until cooked; add cream to the sauce and heat through.
Serve with boiled rice and a wedge of lemon.

CREAMY LEMON TURKEY FRICASSÉE

4 tbsp olive oil
8 turkey breast fillets, sliced
3 onions, sliced
3 garlic cloves, crushed
250ml double cream
3 lemons, zest and juice
handful fresh tarragon, chopped (or 2 tsp dried tarragon)
salt and pepper

Fry the onions in oil in a large pan for about 5 mins.
Fry turkey in batches in a frying pan until slightly brown, adding each batch to the onion pan once cooked.
Add garlic and cook 2-3 minutes.
Add the cream, lemon juice and zest and cook gently for two minutes, or until cooked through.
Stir in tarragon, season to taste and serve.

TURKEY AND MUSHROOM PIE

8 turkey breasts
dried thyme
3 tbsp olive oil
ready rolled flaky pastry
1 egg yolk, beaten with tbsp milk

Coat the meat generously with oil and thyme, cover with foil and cook in oven for **30 mins. at 180C.** (this can be done in the morning).

Make a roux sauce using:
80g butter
80g flour
200ml white wine
200ml cream
juices from the meat (but strain off as much oil as possible)
up to 300ml chicken stock to give a thickish sauce.

To the sauce, mix in:
2 onions, peeled, chopped & fried
4 garlic cloves, fried with the onions (or 4 tsp dried garlic)
600g tinned button mushrooms

Dice the cooked meat into bit-size chunks and spread into a greased dish.
Optionally, add a generous handful of frozen leeks.
Pour over the sauce and mix roughly into the meat.
Cover with pastry, trimming off the excess, and make a few air holes.
Brush the top with beaten egg and bake for about **45 mins at 200C** until golden.

PORK RECIPES

PORK STUFFED WITH APRICOTS (OR PRUNES), COOKED IN CIDER

1.6kg pork (porc roti rolled & tied with string)
150g apricots (or try prunes for a change)
30 ml olive oil
1 litre cider (dry or sweet according to taste)
salt and pepper
2 tbsp cornflour, mixed with a little cold water

Use the handle of a wooden spoon to make a hole down the centre of the entire length of the meat and enlarge with your finger/thumb.
Stuff the apricots into this hole, using your finger/thumb to push into the centre.
Heat the oil in a large pan, season the joint well and brown all over.
Add cider and **simmer for about 1 ½ hours.**
Remove meat from pan, cover with foil and rest before carving.
Pour off excess stock and thicken rest with slaked cornflour; season to taste.
Tip: cut the pork into 2 pieces so they fit side-by-side in the pan; you may need to re-tie the string; the cider should cover at least ¾ of the meat; turn the meat over half-way through cooking.

NORMANDY PORK CHOPS

8 pork chops or steaks
225g mushrooms, sliced
1 litre dry cider
4 apples (peeled, cored and sliced into rings)
4 onions, peeled and thinly sliced
salt and pepper
225g grated cheese (preferably gruyere)
125 g breadcrumbs
1 tbsp cornflour

Gently sweat the onions until soft and then spread them into a buttered, shallow, ovenproof dish.
Season, and add the pork chops; then place the sliced apples on top of the chops, followed by the sliced mushrooms.
Pour on the cider, cover with foil and bake at **190°C for about 40mins**.

Remove foil and pour off excess liquid into a small saucepan and thicken with slaked cornflour to make a cider sauce – season to taste.

Leave the bottom of the chops sitting in some of the liquid, to avoid drying out.
Mix the grated cheese and breadcrumbs with the seasonings, and sprinkle on top of the chops. Bake **20 mins** uncovered.

ROAST PORK

This method enables you to cook the meat in the morning, so that you have plenty of space in the evening for roast potatoes etc. Allowing meat to cool before carving makes it much easier to get nice thin slices.

1.6 kg rolled pork
olive oil
dried sage
salt and pepper

Rub the pork all over with oil, sage, salt and pepper.
Place in a roasting tin, cover with foil and roast very slowly at about **140C for about 2½ hours** until there is absolutely no hint of pink in the juices.
Allow to cool completely before carving. Reheat slices in the oven just before serving.

For gravy, pour the cooking juices into a small pan and skim off excess fat. Add equal quantities of white wine and apple juice to make up to about 500ml. Crumble in a chicken stock cube and bring to the boil. Mix 1 tbsp cornflour with 1 tbsp cold water; add to the pan, stirring continuously and boil to thicken.

LAMB RECIPES

ROAST LAMB

1.5kg lamb, boned roasting joint.
2 cloves garlic, peeled and very thinly sliced
3 tbsp olive oil
1tbsp sunflower oil
1 tbsp butter
1 onion, peeled and finely chopped
600 ml water
2 chicken stock cube
3 tbsp redcurrant jelly
2 tsp ground cumin
2 tsp ground cinnamon
1 tbsp of plain flour
salt and pepper

Pierce the skin of the lamb and spike with the slivers of garlic - do this by inserting a small sharp knife into the lamb vertically and sliding the sliver of garlic down beside the blade into the meat.

Rub over with olive oil and put into the hot oven at **220C for 15 minutes** in a roasting tin to seal and brown the meat.

Meanwhile, put the sunflower oil, butter and onion in a saucepan, cover with a lid and cook over a medium heat until the onion is soft and translucent.

Add the water, stock cube, redcurrant jelly, cumin, cinnamon, salt and pepper to the pan. Bring the liquid to the boil, pour over the meat and cover with foil; put back into the hot oven and after 10 minutes reduce the heat to **190C. Cook for a further 2 hours**.

When the meat is cooked through remove from the dish and wrap tightly in foil and put on the top of the oven in a warm place to rest.

Gravy: pour the cooking liquid into a saucepan and allow the fat to rise to the surface. If there is a lot of fat then spoon most of it off. Allow the remainder to settle back on the surface and sprinkle with flour. Wait for a minute or two and the flour will turn from a white powder to a translucent layer. Stir this into the liquid and bring to the boil, stirring all the time to prevent lumps forming.

If the sauce is still not thick enough (should be the thickness of single cream) the process can be repeated with more flour and any spare fat left on the surface.

LAMB & APRICOT TAGINE

30ml olive oil
1 large onion, chopped
1.25kg boneless lamb, cubed
1 tsp each ground cumin, coriander, cinnamon and paprika (all optional, to taste)
450ml chicken stock
15ml red wine vinegar
15ml runny honey
85g dried apricots, chopped
10g fresh mint, chopped + sprigs for garnish
50g pine nuts, toasted
to garnish: 1 pot natural yoghurt sprig of mint, chopped; salt & pepper

Heat the oil in a large pan and fry the onion until lightly browned.
Add the lamb and stir well, allowing it to seal slightly.
Stir in spices and cook gently for 1 minute.
Add the stock, vinegar, honey and apricots.
Bring to the boil, then lower the heat, cover and simmer for **3+ hours, (or in oven at 140C)** stirring occasionally.
Stir in the chopped mint and pine nuts (keep a few pine nuts for garnishing), and season with salt & pepper to taste; simmer for 15 minutes.
If the sauce seems a bit thin, use slaked cornflour to thicken it.

Meanwhile, mix together the yoghurt & mint and seasoning.
Garnish with sprigs of mint, a drizzle of yoghurt & a few pine nuts and serve with couscous and roasted Mediterranean vegetables

LAMB SHANKS

This is a wonderfully easy recipe, guaranteed to impress your guests, and doesn't spoil with waiting for guests stuck in the snow or traffic on transfer day.

8 lamb shanks
2 bay leaves
1 large onion, sliced
1 bottle red wine
about 700ml stock
salt and pepper

Put all the ingredients in a large roasting tin, with enough liquid to cover the meat.
Cover with foil and cook very slowly at **140C for about 4 hours**, until the meat is really tender.
Pour some of the liquid into a saucepan; add a little port and/or redcurrant jelly, and thicken with slaked cornflour.

BEEF RECIPES

LASAGNE (WITH COLESLAW & GARLIC BREAD)

Some companies scoff at this dish because it sounds cheap (it actually isn't cheap as the French tend to use good quality beef mince) but we've found the guests love it when served at the table with a generous green salad, coleslaw and stacks of garlic bread.

Lasagne is made from alternating layers of meat sauce (ragu), lasagne (pasta) and a cheesy sauce. The 1st time you make this it seems to take forever to prepare but you soon speed up but allow about 40 mins.

For the ragu:
1.5kg minced beef
2 large onions, finely chopped
4 garlic cloves, crushed
300g lardons
400g tinned sliced mushrooms (optional, or use 200g fresh mushrooms)
400g tinned chopped tomatoes
200g tomato puree
2 tbsp olive oil
1 tsp mixed herbs or thyme

Fry the onions and garlic in oil, in a heavy-based big saucepan, for about 10 mins until soft.
Add the lardons and mince and fry gently until mince is browned all over.
Discard any fat that's floating around; with quality mince there'll be very little.
Add the tomatoes & puree & herbs.
Add mushrooms if desired (we don't usually bother); this helps to increase the bulk at low cost!
Some people add a few dollops of chocolate sauce to give a rich brown colour!
Mix well and simmer for about 30 mins.
Tip: *You can make the ragu well ahead of time. When it's cool, any fat rises to the top and can be scooped off easily. You can make it in big batches and freeze it too.*

For the cheese sauce:
100g plain flour
100g butter
~1000ml milk
100g grated emmental
50g grated parmesan
½ tsp grated nutmeg

Make a roux sauce (see earlier); it needs to be fairly thick but still run easily off the spoon.
Add in the cheese and simmer for a few minutes.
A generous helping of grated nutmeg gives it a nice kick.

For the final dish:
400g lasagne sheets
100g grated emmental
50g grated parmesan

Use a large oven-proof dish.
Spoon a layer (about 10mm deep) of ragu into the bottom of the dish.
Spread a layer of lasagne sheets over the ragu.
Spread a generous layer of sauce over the lasagne.
Repeat for another 2 or 3 lots of ragu/lasagne/sauce, depending how deep the dish is.
Finally, sprinkle generous amount of cheese on top.
At this stage you can cover with tinfoil and leave in a cool place until ready to cook.
Cook in oven at **180C for 45mins**; finish under the grill to brown if necessary.
It can be cooked a little ahead of time and put back in the oven just before serving.
The lasagne should be fairly firm, not sloppy, and look fabulous; once you start to serve it though it tends to look messy so we mark out portions with a fish slice or similar and just let the guests *dive into the dish* at the table.

For the coleslaw:
1 small white cabbage
3-4 carrots
1 large onion
1 tbsp brown sugar
1 large handful of raisins or sultanas
~200g mayonnaise

Grate the cabbage, carrots and onion coarsely (use a food-processor if you're lucky enough to have one).
Mix in the sugar, raisins & mayonnaise.

For the garlic bread:
2 baguettes
100g butter
handful chopped fresh parsley
4-6 garlic cloves, crushed

Warm the butter in a microwave until it's very soft & spreadable but not melted.
Mix in the parsley and garlic – I like lots but consider your guests!
Cut each baguette into 2 or 3 pieces and then cut each piece lengthwise (as if you're making sandwiches).
Spread butter generously over each piece of bread.
Slice each *sandwich* into 2cm slices without cutting all the way through the bottom crust; wrap in tinfoil and heat in oven at **180C for 10-15 mins.**
Serve immediately in bread baskets, lined with kitchen roll to absorb any butter; we leave it in the foil to keep warm.

BOEUF BOURGUIGNONNE

1.5 kg braising steak, cut into 5cm cubes
225g lardons
300g onions, cut into segments
2 cloves garlic, chopped
1 bay leaf
2 sprigs fresh thyme or ½ tsp dried
2 tbsp plain flour
700ml red wine
150g mushrooms, sliced
3 tbsp olive oil
salt and pepper

Heat 2 tbsp oil to sizzling and brown the beef a few pieces at a time, remove to a bowl.
Fry onions and lardons in oil.
Return beef to the pan, add flour and stir in well.
Add wine slowly, followed by garlic, seasoning and herbs
Cover and cook for **3 -4 hours at 120C** until just tender.
Add the mushrooms to the casserole and cook (covered) **for another hour.**
The flour should have thickened the juices into a nice gravy but if it's still thin then consider using slaked cornflour, or serve with a slotted spoon to minimise the amount of juice on the plates.

DUCK RECIPES

Duck is delicious but it does have one drawback: copious amounts of fat are exuded during cooking which is messy and does not have the best of smells. It's hard to wash away – water off a duck's back! Never be tempted to throw the fat down the sink or the sink will be well and truly blocked. The best solution that we have found is to pour it into an empty tin, leave to cool (preferably outside where it will solidify) and then throw it out with the rest of your rubbish.

Ideally, leave it on a balcony or windowsill, out of the way of prowling dogs and foxes. We once lost a blender full of stuffing, never to be seen again!

CONFIT DE CANARD

Don't be snobby about '*duck in a can*'; it really is delicious and is always popular with the guests. Readily available in French supermarkets (but not British!), Confit de canard is duck which has been tinned and pre-cooked in its own fat; when cold the fat is solid. Cans usually contain 4, 8 or 12 portions.

8 duck portions
½ jar redcurrant jelly
brown sugar (to taste)
200ml port or red wine
2 tbsp cornflour mixed with water

First, ensure you have all the required roasting trays & utensils to hand, and a large supply of kitchen roll (we use used crumpled, but clean, serviettes because we're mean!). Once you get duck fat on your hands you cannot grip anything else - it's messy and very slippery, so the trick is to keep any mess to the minimum.

Warm the unopened tin(s) for 15 minutes in a sink of hot water to melt some of the fat – when you shake the tin you should be able to hear the fat slopping about! Wipe excess water from the tin.

Stand the tin in a deep roasting tray to catch any drips, cover the tin lid with kitchen roll (in case the internal pressure from heating squirts fat everywhere) & open the tin, completely removing the lid to allow easy access. Now the tricky bit – big tins are quite heavy.

Tip the contents into the tray being careful not to splash the fat everywhere; do not dig it out with any tools as the meat will break apart – remember, it's already been cooked.

Pour any liquid fat back into the tin for disposal and gently scrape away large lumps of solid fat for disposal. Do not try to break apart the pieces of duck at this stage.

Place in a warm oven around **130C** for about 15 minutes.

Careful now – you're handling hot fat & the tray is heavy! Pour off excess fat from the tray into the tin and separate the duck pieces with their skin sides facing upwards.

Crisp the skins in the oven for **20 minutes at 180C.**

Meanwhile, heat the port/wine and jelly together, thicken with cornflour; add sugar as needed

Serve the duck with a little sauce and offer extra sauce in a jug.

Tips: *Beware! Sometimes the tins have less (or more) pieces than advertised – they are really sold by weight. Once separated, you can freeze pieces individually for future use, either to make up the numbers or to crispen for a duck salad. Allow the tin of unwanted duck fat to cool and solidify before disposal in the poubelles. You can roast potatoes in duck fat & they taste superb BUT then you have to clean the oven!*

For pyromaniacs: pour the fat into empty cardboard egg trays and allow to solidify then wrap in a sheet of newspaper – you now have cracking firelighters!

SALMON RECIPES

SALMON WITH PESTO AND PARMESAN

8 salmon fillets
½ jar pesto (red pesto made with sun dried tomatoes is lovely if you can get it)
4 tbsp parmesan
4 heaped tbsp breadcrumbs

Lightly oil a roasting dish and place the salmon fillets in it, skin side down.
Spread about 1 tsp pesto on each piece of salmon.
Combine the parmesan with the breadcrumbs; sprinkle on top of the pesto.
Cover the dish with foil and bake **10-15 minutes at 200C.**

SALMON EN CROUTE

2 rounds puff pastry
½ jar of pesto
800g salmon fillet (or 8 pieces), skinless and boneless
beaten egg to glaze

Lay one round of the pastry onto a lined or greased baking tray and spread the pesto over the surface leaving an uncovered border of 2cm around the edge.
Lay the salmon over the pesto cutting it to fit so that there are no gaps.
Paint the uncovered pastry border with beaten egg.
Cover with the second round of pastry; seal edges by folding bottom edge over top edge (like a Cornish pasty rim). You will have made a round pastry cake shape. Score lines into the surface (do not cut through) and brush with the remaining beaten egg.
Bake at **180C for about 30 minutes** or until the pastry is really well cooked.
Tip: A blend of cream and pesto sauce makes a nice accompaniment.

OVEN BAKED SALMON WITH CHILLI AND GINGER

8 salmon fillets
1-2 fresh red chillis, deseeded and finely chopped
1 piece fresh ginger root (about 10cm), grated or very finely chopped
clear honey
lime juice
salt and pepper
olive oil

Cover the base of a baking tray with baking parchment.
Place the salmon fillets skin-side down on the parchment, leaving a little space between each one; season well and scatter the chilli and ginger over the fillets.
Drizzle a little lime juice, clear honey and olive oil over each fillet.
Cover with foil; bake at **180 C for about 20 minutes**.

SAVOYARDE SPECIALITIES

SAVOYARDE CHICKEN

8 chicken quarters or breasts, skin removed
1 onion
2 cloves
1 carrot, halved lengthways
3 sticks celery (optional)
2 leeks, trimmed (optional)
2 bay leaves
2 sprigs thyme
salt and pepper
100g breadcrumbs
50g parmesan, grated

For the sauce:
75g butter
75g plain flour
500ml chicken stock from the poaching
400ml dry white wine
225ml double cream
150g gruyère cheese, grated
1 tbsp Dijon mustard
50 g tarragon, chopped

Put the chicken pieces in a large saucepan and cover with water.
Stud one of the onions with the cloves and add to the pot along with the remaining vegetables, the herbs and salt to taste.
Bring slowly to the boil, skimming off any scum that comes to the surface.
Reduce the heat to a simmer and **poach gently until cooked** (about 20 mins for breasts or an hour for large quarters).
Once cooked, lift out the chicken pieces; strain the stock and skim off the fat.

To make the sauce, melt the butter in a saucepan, add the flour and cook, stirring, for 1-2 minutes. Gradually stir in the hot chicken stock, the white wine and cream. Keep stirring until thickened. Stir in the cheese, mustard and tarragon. Check the seasoning then simmer, stirring occasionally, for about 20 minutes until smooth and thickened.

Put the chicken pieces in a greased gratin dish and pour over the sauce.
Sprinkle with the breadcrumbs and parmesan.
Bake for **20-25 at 220C** minutes until golden brown and bubbling around the edges.

TARTIFLETTE

2 kg potatoes, peeled
3 cloves garlic, crushed
250ml white wine
350ml cream
3 tbsp cornflour
2 onions, sliced
30ml olive oil
500g lardons
1 reblochon cheese (these come in rounds about 6 inch diameter; sometimes called tartiflette cheese)

Boil the potatoes for 10-15 until slightly soft then drain & cool them enough to handle (do not overcook)
Boil the garlic in the wine for a few minutes then stir in the cream and thicken (like double cream) with slaked cornflour.
Heat the olive oil and soften the onions for about 10 mins, then add the lardons and cook for about 10 mins. then drain the juices & mix them into the wine sauce.
Slice the potatoes into ~4-5mm slices and make 1 layer in a greased baking dish.
Arrange half of the lardon mix on top then pour over half of the sauce.
Make another layer of potatoes then lardons and sauce.
Cut the reblochon in half horizontally and place on top of the potatoes, rind side up (genuine reblochon has an edible label embedded in the skin/crust which looks strange to "British" guests, so we cut this out before cooking).
Bake at **180C for about 45 minutes**, until the cheese has melted and the mixture is bubbling hot with a brownish crust.

Tip: *See the Soup section for uses of any leftovers. In the UK, if you cannot get reblochon then use camembert with an extra sprinkling of strong cheddar.*

VEGETABLES

As a rule of thumb, allow 100-150g of vegetables per person, assuming you're serving two types with the meal, but see individual recipes below.

When boiling vegetables, a simple rule of thumb is that root vegetables (they grow under the ground), e.g. potatoes & carrots, are placed in cold water, whilst those that grow above, e.g. beans & peas, are placed in boiling water.

After peeling root vegetables put them in a pan of cold water otherwise they will tend to discolour quite quickly; they take longer to cook at altitude – allow up to 1 hour at 2000m; cutting into smallish pieces will speed up cooking.

Spring cabbage, broccoli etc take 5-10 mins. – cut/chop leaves/florets into bite-size pieces and plunge into boiling water.

Most frozen vegetables are already cooked/blanched and only need heating in boiling water: thaw the vegetables during the day sealed in their bag; place in boiling water and return to boil; then strain and serve.

Most vegetables benefit from a little salt during cooking, including frozen ones. Peas taste nice with a little sugar too.

Sometimes you may wish to 'family serve' vegetables in large pre-heated dishes which you place in the middle of the table for guests to serve themselves. When family serving, provide all vegetables at each end of the table so that all guests can easily reach all the vegetables.

Freeze any leftovers to make Soupe Du Jour – see earlier.

OLIVE OIL & SEA SALT BAKED POTATOES (HASSELBACK)

Note: these are named after the Stockholm restaurant that first served them in the 1700s; *hassel* means hazel or nut-like in Swedish.

16 medium or 24 small potatoes (not peeled)
~30 ml olive oil
coarse sea salt

Make downwards cuts about 3/4 of the way through the potatoes, about 4-5mm apart; an easy way to do this is to put each small potato in the bowl of a wooden spoon, or between two chopping boards for medium ones, so that you cannot cut all the way through.

Place in a roasting dish, drizzle olive oil over each potato and sprinkle liberally with salt.

Roast for about **60 minutes at 200C,** basting every 20 minutes & adding a little more salt, until the outside of the potatoes are brown and crispy and the insides are soft.

ROASTED SWEET POTATO CHIPS

Cut sweet potatoes into large chips or wedges.

Place in an oiled roasting tin and drizzle with oil (either sunflower or olive); toss to coat the chips with oil.

Roast for about **40 mins at 190C,** stirring once during cooking.

GRATIN DAUPHINOIS

1 kg potatoes, peeled & very thinly sliced
25g butter
about 1 litre double cream
3 cloves garlic, crushed
salt and pepper
250g grated emmental

Arrange potato slices in layers with garlic and seasoning, in a well buttered dish.
Pour cream over to just cover the potatoes, dot with butter, cover with foil and **bake about 2 hours at 150 C.**
Remove foil, sprinkle with cheese and bake at about **180C for 20 minutes.**
Tip: *Line dish with baking parchment to minimise washing up. You can cook the potatoes in the morning, leave in the oven (turned off) all day, then top with cheese and finish just before dinner. Before topping with cheese, spoon out any excess liquid, or add milk if the potatoes are too dry.*

POTATOES BOULANGERE

This recipe takes less time to prepare (no peeling) and it cooks more quickly at a higher temperature than the dauphinois potatoes.

1200 g potatoes, thinly sliced, no need to peel
1 large onion, sliced
50ml white wine
350 ml milk
50g butter
salt and pepper

Arrange potatoes in layers in a well buttered dish with onions and seasoning.
Heat wine and milk and pour over, dot with butter and bake **45 minutes at 180C.**

MUSTARD MASH

2 kg potatoes, peeled and cut into chunks (smaller chunks cook quicker)
~100 ml cream or milk
50g butter
2-3 tbsp mustard (we use a mixture of Dijon and grainy)
salt and pepper

Boil the potatoes in lightly salted water until tender (this will probably take about 40 minutes) then drain.
Mash roughly then add butter and milk/cream and mustard then mash thoroughly; season to taste.

LYONNAISE POTATOES

1.2 kg potatoes (washed and cut into 1 cm slices; peeling optional)
3 tbsp olive oil
4 onions, thinly sliced
2 cloves garlic, finely chopped
50g butter
salt and pepper
1 tablespoon finely chopped fresh parsley

Place sliced potatoes in a pan; cover with water and bring to the boil; boil 5 minutes, then drain and set aside.
Meanwhile, fry onions in hot oil until golden brown (about 10 minutes).
Add garlic and continue frying until garlic is soft (about 5 mins).
Grease an ovenproof dish with half the butter; cover bottom of pan with 1/3 of potatoes. Season well.
Cover potatoes with 1/2 of onion mixture.
Repeat layers until all ingredients are used, ending with potatoes and seasoning.
Dot with remaining butter.
Bake at **200C for 30-40 minutes**, or until potatoes are tender and browned on top.
Remove from oven and use a spatula to carefully transfer potatoes to a serving platter. Sprinkle with chopped parsley just before serving.

SWEET POTATO ROSTIS

2 large sweet potatoes, peeled & grated
4 tbsp corn flour
1 tbsp fresh parsley, chopped
2 apples, grated
3 spring onions, finely chopped
salt & pepper
30ml olive oil

Combine all ingredients except the oil in a large bowl.
Heat the oil in a large frying pan; take a large spoonful of the rosti mixture, place it in the pan and press down on it well and shape into a burger so that it will stick together as it cooks.
Cook several at once, allowing enough room to be able to turn them over.
Cook for about 10 minutes on each side until they are golden brown and also hold together well.

These can be cooked in advance then put under a hot grill for a few minutes to reheat them —this will help to crisp them up too.

PAN FRIED LEEKS

4-5 leeks
50 ml sunflower oil

Rinse the leeks well. Cut the stem end off and any dried leaf tips of the dark green tops. Slice in half lengthwise. Rinse again to remove any dirt from the inside of the leeks. Slice the leeks crosswise to make *tubes* of 2-3cms in length.

Heat the oil in a large pan; add the leeks and adjust the heat to be hot enough to wilt the leeks and brown them only very lightly. Stir occasionally. They are done when the dark green tops are easily cut with a dinner knife - about 15 minutes.

COUSCOUS WITH ROASTED MEDITERRANEAN VEGETABLES

6 courgettes
2 aubergines
2 peppers – red or yellow
3 onions, peeled & quartered
10 cloves garlic, peeled
60ml olive oil
2 tsp dried rosemary
salt & pepper

Cut the courgettes into 2cm chunks, quarter and slice the aubergines and cut the peppers into bite size pieces; add onions & garlic.
Place all the vegetables on a roasting tray, sprinkle with salt, pepper and dried rosemary and drizzle generously with olive oil.
Roast in a hot oven (about 200C) for 35 – 45 minutes, until the vegetables are soft and slightly charred.

Accompaniment:
400g couscous
30ml olive oil
salt & pepper
 boiling water
When the vegetables are ready, use a jug to measure the couscous into a bowl with a little olive oil and some salt & pepper. Pour the same volume of boiling water over the couscous, cover and leave for **4-5 minutes**. Stir with a fork to loosen the grains, then mix in the roasted vegetables with all of their cooking juices.
Serve immediately.

VEGETABLE PILAU RICE

This recipe makes no pretence at being authentic, but it is easy, foolproof and tasty!

800g basmati or long grain rice
2 medium onions, finely chopped
2 red peppers, chopped
2 tbsp oil
1 dessertspoon curry powder
1 dessertspoon turmeric
1 cup frozen peas
100g sultanas
100g salted peanuts or cashew nuts

Cook the rice in boiling salted water with the turmeric for 12 minutes, adding the frozen peas half way through.
Meanwhile, fry the onion in the oil for around 5 minutes until softened; add the pepper and cook for another few minutes; add the curry powder and cook for a couple more minutes.
Stir in the nuts and sultanas.
Drain the rice/peas and rinse with boiling water; add to the onion/pepper mixture and mix well before serving.

ORANGE BRAISED RED CABBAGE

pinch cumin seeds
3 tbsp olive oil
1 red onion, finely sliced
1 red cabbage, sliced as finely as possible
100ml orange juice
100ml balsamic vinegar
150g raisins
pepper

Dry fry the cumin seeds for a minute or two to release the flavour; add the oil and onion and cook gently for about 5 minutes until the onion is soft but not brown.
Add the cabbage and stir to cover in oil, then continue cooking for another 10 minutes.

Add the orange juice, vinegar, raisins and pepper to taste.
Cover with a close fitting lid and cook for about 45 minutes, stirring occasionally.
Tip: you can make this in large batches as it freezes well; then thaw thoroughly and re-heat in a pan with more orange juice.

SAVOURY SPRING CABBAGE

100g butter
1 large young cabbage, finely shredded
2 onions, skinned and finely chopped
150g lardons
2 good pinches of grated nutmeg

Heat the butter in a large saucepan and fry onion and lardons for 5 mins.
Add all remaining ingredients, cover pan and cook very gently for about 20 minutes, until the cabbage is just tender, shaking the pan frequently.
Garnish with flaked almonds, as desired.

'VICHY' CARROTS

Vichy carrots originated in the town of Vichy and are traditionally cooked in Vichy mineral water, then glazed with butter and sugar.
This recipe uses white wine and rosemary - definitely an upmarket version! It is best to cook the carrots until soft before adding the wine, or the carrots will take ages to soften.

1 kg carrots, peeled and sliced diagonally
sprig of rosemary (or 1 tsp dried rosemary)
100ml white wine
50g sugar
pinch of salt
50g butter

Place the sliced carrots in a saucepan with the rosemary, half the sugar, salt and enough water to cover. Boil for about 40 minutes until the carrots are soft; pour off the liquid and stir in the remaining sugar, butter and wine; cook gently for 5-10 minutes until the wine has reduced and the carrots are glazed.

OVEN ROASTED ROOT VEGETABLES

2 onions, peeled and cut into quarters (leave root end intact)
4 potatoes, scrubbed and cut lengthwise into 1cm thick slices
2 turnips (~600g), peeled and cut into eighths
3 large carrots, peeled and cut into 8cm lengths (cut thickest pieces in half lengthwise)
2 large parsnips, peeled and cut into 8cm lengths (cut thickest pieces into halves or quarters lengthwise)
2 medium butternut squashes, peeled, halved, seeded, and cut into 8-by-2cm pieces
10 to 20 garlic cloves, loose papery outer skins removed, inner skins left on
2 sweet potatoes, peeled and cut into 8-by-2cm pieces
about ¾ cup extra-virgin olive oil
1 tbsp coarse salt, plus more to taste
½ tbsp freshly ground black pepper, plus more to taste
handful fresh rosemary

Put all vegetables (including garlic) except sweet potatoes into a very large bowl; put sweet potatoes in a separate bowl. Drizzle both bowls generously with olive oil and sprinkle with salt and pepper. Toss gently with your hands to coat with oil.
Spread vegetables onto a large baking sheet and sprinkle with rosemary.
Roast vegetables **at 200C for 15 minutes;** stir gently if they are sticking.
Add the sweet potatoes and continue roasting, stirring occasionally for **another hour** or so, until the vegetables are browned and tender.

WILTED SPINACH

1kg spinach
50g butter or olive oil
salt and pepper
Heat the oil or butter in a large frying pan; add the spinach and stir-fry until wilted (about 5 minutes). Season to taste.

DESSERTS

LEMON POSSET

700ml double cream
150g caster sugar
3 large lemons (zest and juice)

Place cream, zest and sugar in pan over low heat until sugar dissolves; bring to boil (CARE) and simmer for 3 minutes.
Remove from heat and cool for about 5 minutes.
Whisk in juice.
Strain into a jug, pour into glasses or ramekins and **refrigerate for 1-2 hours**.
Serve with *langues des chats* or similar dessert biscuits.

BANANA BAKEWELL

1 pack shortcrust pastry
2-3 heaped tspns apricot jam
3 bananas
100g soft butter
100g caster sugar
1 large egg
100g plain flour
1 tsp raising agent

Line flan tin with pastry.
Spread with jam and one sliced banana.
Cream the butter and sugar, beat in the egg and 2 mashed bananas and stir in flour.
Spread over bananas in tin.
Bake at **220 C for 15 minutes**, reduce temperature and cook for a further **20 minutes at 170C**.
Serve with vanilla ice cream

CARAMELISED APPLES

8 eating apples
100g butter
100g demerara sugar
1 tsp ground cinnamon
50g flaked almonds
50ml orange or apple juice

Peel and core the apples and cut in half through the core so that each half has a hole.
Use a little of the butter to grease a large shallow ovenproof dish. Put the apples in the dish, cut-side up. Dot the butter all over the apples; sprinkle with the sugar, cinnamon and almonds. Sprinkle the orange juice around the dish.
Bake at **200C for 30-35 minutes** until the apples are tender and golden.
Serve with vanilla ice cream.

BAKED BANANAS

8 bananas
2 tbsp finely chopped root ginger
4 tbsp clear honey

Slice bananas into 4 on the slant, sprinkle with ginger and honey, cover with foil and bake **12-15 minutes at 190 C.**
Serve with ice cream.

BLACK FOREST PAVLOVA

Pavlova is a national dish of Australia and New Zealand but everyone loves it. This dessert is stunning to look at before it is cut into portions, but can look a bit of a mess once it is served, so pick a guest to cut and serve it at the table!

For the meringue:
4 egg whites
200g caster sugar
20g cocoa powder, sieved
5ml wine vinegar
40g dark chocolate, finely chopped

For the topping:
425ml double cream
200g dark chocolate
200g forest fruits

Preheat the oven to 170C and line a baking tray with greaseproof paper.
Whisk the whites & vinegar until stiff.
Add sugar and whisk for 2 seconds.
Sprinkle on the cocoa and chocolate then gently fold everything together until thoroughly mixed (but do not over mix).
Spread onto the baking tray to make a circle.
Place in the oven, then immediately turn the temperature down to **130C and cook for 60 minutes**.
When it's ready it should look crisp around the edges. Ideally turn off the oven and leave the meringue inside to cool overnight or for several hours.
Tips: *ensure your mixing bowl & utensils are absolutely clean and dry; you should be able to hold the bowl upside down over your head when it's whisked enough; fold in the cocoa etc with a metal or silicone spoon to ensure the captured air is not released (by the surface reaction of plastics and protein).*

Make some chocolate sauce by melting 75g chocolate with 125g cream; simmer for 2-3 minutes.
Whip the rest of the cream and chop the chocolate.
Cover the meringue with cream, drizzle with sauce and sprinkle with chopped chocolate and forest fruits.

TARTE TATIN

A French classic for which you need a shallow, heavy based pan which can go in the oven (we use an old frying pan which the handle had fallen off)

3 large apples (peeled, cored, sliced into 12 segments per apple and ideally left uncovered for 2-3 hours to brown)
1 sheet puff pastry to fit pan
50g unsalted butter, thinly sliced
50g soft brown sugar mixed with 1/2 tsp cinnamon

Thoroughly butter the pan and then lay the butter slices in the bottom the pan.
Arrange the apple slices overlapped to make a neat circle and infill the centre with more pieces.
Sprinkle over the sugar.
Cook on the hob on medium heat until the butter and sugar have melted, forming a light sticky caramel (about 15 minutes). Remove the pan from the heat.
Lay the pastry over the apples and fold in the edges if necessary to make a crust.
Bake for 20 minutes at 180C until the pastry is brown and crisp.
Remove from oven, free the pastry from the pan with a knife if needed, cover with a large plate and flip the over so that the tarte is apple side up! Any pieces that stick in the pan can be placed back on the tarte.
Dust generously with icing sugar; serve warm with vanilla ice cream or pouring cream.
Tip: it's best to cook this dish just prior to serving.

CITRUS APPLE FLAN WITH SYLLABUB

This is really tangy and surprises many guests.
6 medium apples, cored
1 sheet short pastry
4 eggs
225g sugar
1 lemon, zest & juice
125g butter, melted
2 tbsp brown sugar

Coarsely grate the apples and leave in a sieve to drain – the longer the better to give a nice brown colour.
Line the greased flan tin then lay the pastry inside and gently tease it into position, cut off any excess, prick base with fork several times, and chill for 10 mins.
Beat the eggs, sugar, lemon juice & zest with a hand whisk then whisk in the melted butter.
Squeeze the excess moisture from the apples then add to the mix and mix thoroughly before tipping into the flan case and spreading evenly.
Sprinkle with brown sugar.
Bake 40-45 minutes at 180C until golden brown and fairly firm.
Tip: depending on your oven, you may wish to blind-bake the pastry a little first.

Allow to cool and serve warm with **syllabub**:
500ml cream
250g sugar
2 lemons, zest & juice
8 tbsp sweet white wine
Whisk all ingredients together until thick but floppy. This can be made in larger batches, then frozen and served like ice cream.

JAFFA PUDDING

Imagine hot melted Jaffa cakes! The recipe seems bizarre and takes a fair amount of preparation but you get faster each time you make it. It's worth it.

250g plain flour
4 tsp raising agent
140g caster sugar
50g cocoa
2 oranges, zest and juice
100g butter, melted
3 eggs
150ml milk
100g plain (or orange flavoured) chocolate, broken into chunks

Mix flour, raising agent, sugar, cocoa and orange zest in a large bowl.
Whisk juice, butter, milk and eggs in a jug; add to bowl; mix till smooth, stir in chocolate and scrape into a greased 2 litre baking dish.

Mix together:
200g muscovado sugar
25g cocoa
300ml boiling water
Pour all over cake mix and bake **30 minutes at 160C**

Tip: *get everything ready to go beforehand but don't mix it all up until you're ready to cook.*

WHITE CHOCOLATE CHEESECAKE WITH RASPBERRY COULIS

400g "Spritz"(shortcake) biscuits
100g butter
300g cream cheese
200g white chocolate
about 100ml cream (will depend on type of cream so add slowly)
250g frozen raspberries, defrosted

Crumb the biscuits, melt the butter and mix the two together. Press the biscuit mixture into a greased flan tin and place in the fridge.
Melt the white chocolate and mix in the cream cheese, then enough cream to make a mousse like consistency. Stir thoroughly to ensure the mix is lump free and well blended.
Pour over the biscuit base and leave to set in the **fridge for at least two hours**.
Meanwhile press the raspberries through a sieve to make a coulis or pouring sauce; sweeten to taste with icing sugar.
Serve a slice of cheesecake drizzled with coulis, garnished with a mint leaf and one or two raspberries.

LEMON & LIME CHEESECAKE

400g "Spritz" (shortcake) biscuits
100g butter

For the filling:
450g cream cheese
juice of a lemon
1 tbsp icing sugar, sieved

For the citrus curd:
juice & grated rind of 2 lemons & 1 lime
3 eggs, well beaten
50g unsalted butter, cubed
300g sugar
strips of lemon & lime rind, for garnish

Crumb the biscuits by placing in a strong plastic bag and bashing with a rolling pin.
Melt the butter in a saucepan (don't let it get too hot) and mix in the crumbs.
Press the biscuit mixture into a greased flan tin and place in the fridge until set.
To make the filling, mix cream cheese, icing sugar and lemon juice, smooth over base and leave to set in fridge.
For the citrus curd, place all the ingredients together in a bowl over a pan of simmering water, stir until the sugar has dissolved, then stir from time to time until the curd thickens. This will take about 25-30 minutes. Pour into a cold bowl, cover and leave to cool slightly. While still slightly warm, pour over the cheese filling.
Chill for at least 2 hours then serve, garnished with lemon & lime rind.

LEMON TART

1 round shortcrust pastry
6 eggs
225g caster sugar
125g unsalted butter, in pieces
finely grated rind of 3 lemons
150ml freshly squeezed lemon juice

Line a flan tin with the pastry.
Bake blind (see earlier).

To make the filling, place all ingredients in a bowl over a pan of simmering water. Whisk until well blended and continue stirring until the mixture thickens slightly - just enough to coat the back of a wooden spoon.
Pour the filling into the pastry case and bake in the oven for **25 mins at 180C** or until set.
Allow to cool slightly.
Serve warm or cold, cut into wedges, decorated with shreds of peel and a dusting of icing sugar. Accompany with crème fraiche.
Tip: *microwaving cold lemons for 10-20 seconds enables more juice to be extracted.*

BANANA BRIOCHE AND BUTTER PUDDING

3/4 loaf of pre-sliced brioche
75g butter, softened
100g caster sugar
6 eggs
~500ml cream
2 sliced bananas
handful raisins &/or sultanas
2 tbsp rum
icing sugar to dust

Put the raisins in a small saucepan with the rum, bring to the boil and turn off. This plumps up the raisins and gives the pudding a little kick!

Butter each piece of brioche thinly but thoroughly with the softened butter on both sides.

In a bowl, whisk together the sugar and eggs till pale and fluffy, then add the cream and whisk until smooth.

Soak each piece of bread thoroughly in the egg mixture then make a bottom layer of bread in the (greased) dish, ensuring all the gaps are filled up with bread pieces; use your fingers to mould it softly like putty.

Spread out the majority of the raisins and all the sliced banana over the bottom layer and pour in the warm rum. Make a top layer of soaked bread then sprinkle with a few raisins.

Pour over the rest of your egg mixture, using your fingers to pat down the bread to make sure it soaks up all the liquid. A bit of liquid should remain but not swimming in it!

Stand for 10 minutes, after which there should still be a bit of surplus liquid (add more if not!) then bake **at 180C for around 35 minutes** or until the custard has set around the outside but is just slightly wobbly in the centre. It should look golden brown. Allow it to cool a bit, and firm up slightly. Serve with a dusting of icing sugar and vanilla ice cream.

Tip: cut the butter into smallish pieces and melt in microwave (covered with kitchen roll to catch any spatter) then place 6 slices or so on the work surface and pour butter over them and spread with knife – it's the fastest way to butter a loaf!

APRICOT CRUMBLE

2 x 450g cans of apricots
350g plain flour
1.5 tsp raising agent
125g butter (room temp)
200g sugar (ideally soft brown but white will do)

Sieve flour and raising agent, rub in butter then stir in sugar.

Place apricots in a baking dish, cover with crumble and bake for **30 minutes at 180C.**

Serve with pouring cream or ice cream.

MANGO (OR APRICOT) FOOL

3 large ripe mangoes (or use a large tin of mangoes, or apricots), puréed
150ml double cream, whipped
120ml thick yoghurt
1tbsp icing sugar

Combine all ingredients; serve in glasses decorated with mango slices or chopped pistachios.

STICKY TOFFEE PUDDING WITH ORANGE TOFFEE SAUCE

1 mug pitted dried dates, chopped
1 mug hot water
75g butter
1 mug plain flour
1 tsp raising agent
1 ½ tsp cinnamon
1 tsp ground ginger
¾ mug soft brown sugar
3 eggs, beaten

Prepare the ramekins by greasing well with butter, then lining with baking parchment (only if you plan to turn out the puddings to serve!) Alternatively, grease a shallow baking dish (about 30 x20 cm).
Microwave or cook the dates with the hot water until soft and mushy; drain any excess water; stir in the butter and set aside.
Put the flour, raising agent and spices in another bowl and mix, then stir in the brown sugar.
Add the eggs to the date mixture and mix well, then fold into the dry ingredients.
Pour into ramekins and bake for about **25 minutes at 170C** until a knife comes out clean.

For the **orange sauce**:
1 mug creme fraiche
1 mug soft brown sugar
1 orange, grated rind and juice
Combine sauce ingredients in small pan and heat gently until smooth.
Turn out puddings onto warm plate, pour the sauce over and serve with crème fraiche.

PETIT POTS AU CHOCOLAT

Smooth and sumptuous – the ultimate chocolate pudding! It is very rich, so the portions should be small. Espresso cups are ideal.

400 ml milk
200 ml double cream
100g caster sugar
1 heaped tbsp cornflour
50g cocoa powder (sieved)
3 tbsp boiling water
3 egg yolks
1 tsp vanilla extract
100g dark chocolate, finely chopped

Warm the milk and cream.
Place the sugar, cocoa and cornflour in a pan; add the boiling water and whisk to a paste.
Whisk in egg yolks, one at a time, followed by the milk, cream and vanilla.
Scrape sides of pan back into the mix and cook on low heat until simmering, whisking for about 5 minutes until mix thickens.
Take off heat and mix in the chocolate.
Pour into espresso cups or small glasses; to prevent a skin forming, cover the surface with clingfilm ensuring the film is in contact with the chocolate.
Once cool, **refrigerate for several hours** but remove 20 minutes before serving.
Serve with a *cigarette russe* or other dessert biscuit.

FOREST FRUIT CRISP

200g butter, melted
100g oats
50g flaked almonds
50g sunflower seeds
120g plain flour
120g soft brown sugar
800g fruits of the forest
1 tbsp cornflour
75 g caster sugar

Place the fruit into a shallow baking dish and sprinkle with caster sugar and cornflour; stir to mix. Combine all other dry ingredients; stir in melted butter and spoon over berry mix. Bake for 25 minutes at 200C.

TIRAMISU

This recipe for the classic rich Italian dessert does not include raw eggs (most do!).

300ml strong black coffee, cooled
100ml Tia Maria, Baileys liqueur or brandy
300g sponge fingers
500g mascarpone
100ml double cream
100g caster sugar
1 tbsp cocoa powder

Mix the coffee and liqueur in a bowl; soak half the sponge fingers until they are damp but not too soggy, and use them to line a deep dish about 20x10cm , e.g. a loaf tin.
Whip together the cream, sugar and mascarpone. Spread half this mixture over the sponge fingers.
Repeat with another layer of sponge followed by the cream mixture.
Cover the dish with clingfilm and leave in the fridge for at least 6 hours.
Just before serving, remove from the dish onto a plate and dredge with sieved cocoa powder.
Tip: Line the tin with clingfilm and it's easier to extract the tiramisu when ready. Serve at the table so the guests can see how great it looks before it's cut.

CHOCOLATE MOUSSE

This is a mousse without raw eggs (and very easy too).

150g marshmallows, chopped into small pieces
50g butter, cut into small pieces
250g dark chocolate, chopped
60ml hot water
300ml double cream
1 tsp vanilla extract

Heat the marshmallows, butter, chocolate and water gently in a pan until melted and smooth; remove from heat.
Whip cream with vanilla till thick, then fold into cooling chocolate mixture.
Pour into glasses, espresso cups or ramekins and chill for about an hour until set.
Tip: Use scissors to cut the marshmallows & dip the scissors often into hot water to stop them sticking.

QUICK CHOCOLATE SAUCE

For a rich sauce:
75g dark chocolate
1 tbsp golden syrup
125 ml double cream
1 tsp vanilla

OR from store cupboard ingredients
2 tbsp cocoa
4 tbsp golden syrup or honey
50g butter, chilled and diced
100 ml milk
1 tsp vanilla

In either case, blend all ingredients in a small pan, stirring continuously until melted; simmer for 2-3 minutes.

BUTTERSCOTCH SAUCE

100g demerara sugar
100g butter
100g golden syrup
150 ml milk (or cream if posh)

Heat sugar, butter and syrup gently to melt, then boil until soft ball stage (i.e. when small amount is dropped into cold water it forms a ball).
Cool slightly then slowly add the milk.

GALETS AUX FRUITS CONFIT

200g chocolate (dark, milk or white)
100g mixed dried fruits and nuts (e.g. apricots, almonds, walnuts, cranberries, pineapple…)

Melt chocolate and drop spoonfuls onto baking parchment.
Arrange fruit and nuts on melted chocolate; cool and serve with mousses, ice cream or coffee

SPECIAL DIETARY REQUIREMENTS

Special dietary requirements range from life threatening conditions (e.g. severe nut allergy) through lifestyle choices (e.g. vegetarians) right down to plain fussiness (I don't eat onions but shallots are fine!).

Without a doubt they make the chalet host's job more difficult but all guests deserve to be treated equally. In a domestic kitchen, just rustling up a stuffed pepper can wreck your menu plan as you fight for space in the oven.

Guests with medical conditions will often bring special foods with them (e.g. sweeteners, soya milk, rice cakes) or give you advance warning so that you can buy them.

You will usually be advised in advance when you have guests with special dietary requirements; most will be pleased to discuss their needs with you, and will be very grateful for the extra effort you make. If possible, contact them before they arrive to find out exactly what they can and cannot eat.

It's best to ask everyone on their first evening about any violent dislikes to avoid problems later in the week. Normally you've already done the shopping for these guests so late surprises are… a challenge! But beware of allowing everyone just to pick and choose what they fancy – a chalet menu is essentially fixed.

In our kitchen we have a whiteboard (or piece of paper) with a list of *specials* for the week, e.g. "1 vegetarian, 2 gluten-free", 1 dairy-free; then each day we write up the impact on that day's menu, e.g.
- Starter: Seafood Gratin – 10 OK, 1 mushroom (instead of fish), 1 no cheese
- Main: Lasagne – 8 OK, 3 jacket potatoes with meat sauce 2 with cheese topping, 1 jacket with chickpea tagine
- Dessert: Pavlova & fruit & cream – 11 OK, 1 meringue & fruit

Don't forget to consider any vegetables and sauces.

One company that we know of charges a supplement to guests with special requirements and this money goes to the host to compensate for the inconvenience – cracking idea!!

Many of the recipes in the main section can be adapted for specific needs, and there are plenty of internet sites with additional recipes.

FOOD ALLERGIES AND INTOLERANCES

Food allergies and intolerances must be taken very seriously. People have died after being given false reassurance that a dish is free of a food they are sensitive to.

When someone asks if a dish contains a certain food, you must check all the ingredients, including stock cubes, sauces, garnishing and salad dressing too. This isn't easy when the ingredients might be in French! Larger companies will have a resident expert. Never guess – ask for help.

Don't be perturbed if they repeatedly ask you what you're cooking. If they have a serious problem they may inspect each crumb of food. Between you, you'll get it right so don't worry and don't make them feel awkward (although sometimes you could murder the "fakes").

Food Allergies

Sufferers with a severe food allergy may have life-threatening reactions called anaphylaxis, often within minutes of eating even minute amounts. If they are not treated quickly, they may die.

The foods most commonly associated with severe reactions are peanuts, tree nuts (e.g. walnuts, almonds, hazelnuts, cashew, Brazils) and seeds (e.g. poppy, sesame).

Food Intolerances

Food Intolerances are not the same as food allergies and are not normally life-threatening. However, eating foods you have an intolerance to can make you feel ill or affect long-term health.

Common allergens

Wheat free - A wheat free diet excludes all products derived from wheat; obvious candidates are flour, bread, cakes, pastry, pasta and couscous. Wheat products may also be 'hidden' in many processed foods such as stock cubes, ice cream, sauces, sausages and beer.

It is best to discuss a wheat intolerance with the guest to find out what is allowed.

Permitted forms of starch usually include cornflour, potatoes, rice, soya flour and oats. Obviously any recipes using pastry will not be suitable; these can easily be replaced by a salad or plain grilled food. Fruit desserts are often OK; (try lemon posset, toffee apples, mango fool, fruit salad and also choc pots). Afternoon tea causes the most hassle; flapjacks, fruit and nut bars and flourless chocolate brownies are all wheat free.

www.wheat-free.org has an good range of recipes.

Gluten free - A gluten free diet is like a wheat free diet with extra forbidden foods. People on a gluten free diet often have celiac disease (an auto-immune disease) and cannot tolerate any form of gluten.

Gluten is found in rye and barley as well as wheat; some celiacs cannot eat oats either.

Wine, brandy, cider, sherry, port and rum do not contain gluten, but some vineyards use a flour paste to caulk the oak barrels in which wine is aged, so some celiacs may wish to exercise caution.

Usually: cornflakes are OK; use marmite instead of stocks; use cornflour to thicken sauces; flapjacks are OK.

www.ozemail.com.au has an extensive range of recipes.

Dairy free / lactose intolerant - People on a dairy free diet avoid cheese, milk, butter, yogurt, cream, cottage cheese and crème fraîche. Soya products (milk, spreads and cream) can be substituted for the dairy products.

www.bbc.co.uk/food/recipes has a good section on dairy free catering.

Peanuts (groundnuts) - used in a lot of foods including sauces, cakes, desserts, Thai and Indonesian dishes, Coronation chicken. Be aware of peanut flour and groundnut oil.

Tree Nuts - including walnuts, pecans, cashews, almonds, Brazil nuts and hazelnuts. Found in many foods, including sauces, crackers, desserts, bread, ice cream. Be aware of nut oils, pesto, ground almonds and marzipan.

Eggs - used in hundreds of dishes including cakes, sauces, pasta, mousses, and quiche. Egg is often used to bind products too, such as burgers, or as a basting agent, for example brushed onto pastry. Some dressings include egg too, like mayonnaise and Hollandaise.

Fish pizzas, salads, dressings, relishes, and sauces may include fish as an ingredient, particularly anchovies. Fish sauce is also commonly used in Thai dishes.

Shellfish - There are a variety of different shellfish that sufferers may need to avoid, including scampi, prawns, mussels, squid and crab. In addition, shrimp paste and oyster sauce are often found in Chinese and Thai dishes and sauces.

Soya - may be served as tofu, beancurd, soya flour, soya milk or a textured soya protein. It is in many foods, including sauces, vegetarian products like veggie burgers, ice cream, other desserts, and even some meat products.

Sesame seeds - often used to garnish bread or bread products. Sesame oil can also be also used for cooking or in some dressings. Tahini is a sesame paste used in some Mediterranean dishes, including hummus.

Celery - People with a celery allergy may also react to celeriac. Both may be used in salads or soups, or may simply be served as a vegetable. Beware of celery salt, used to season foods, particularly soups and meat products, and celery seeds which are sometimes used as a spice ingredient.

Mustard - People with mustard allergy will react to any food that is derived from the mustard plant including mustard powder, liquid mustard, mustard oil, mustard leaves, seeds and flowers. It is often used in salad dressings, curries, soups, marinades, sauces, gravy and meat products.

Sulphur dioxide - Some asthma sufferers react to sulphur dioxide. It is used as a preservative in a lot of foods, particularly meat products like sausages, soft drinks, dried fruit like apricots and vegetables. Sulphur dioxide is also found in beers and wine.

Vegan

Catering for vegans in a chalet environment poses a bit of a challenge! But a challenge is something to rise to!

Vegans do not eat any foods derived from living or dead animals - no meat of any kind (no red meat, poultry, white meat, fish etc.), no dairy products (cows, sheep, goats etc.), no eggs, no honey, nor any other animal products (no gelatin, cochineal, etc.)

Vegans enjoy all kinds of plant foods - like fruits, vegetables, grains, nuts, seeds, legumes (beans, lentils and split peas) - and fungi (mushrooms, yeasts), and food made from these. They will eat tofu and soya milk.

Some of the vegetarian recipes are suitable for vegans (Chick pea tagine and patties, chilli beans, stir fried tofu). Others can be adapted by using soya products in place of dairy.

www.veganvillage.co.uk has a good range of vegan recipes.

Diabetic

People with diabetes are unable to absorb glucose from the blood stream, usually because they do not produce enough insulin. Glucose is contained in carbohydrates, particularly sugars, so that diabetics need to control the amount of sugar in their diet. Some diabetics are able to control the condition by following a careful diet; others need to inject insulin regularly.

Most diabetics are well aware of the foods they are able to eat, and many will be able to eat most starters and main meals without any special modifications. However, cakes and desserts, being typically high in sugar, will cause more of a problem.

The diabetic fruit cake in the cakes section does not contain any added sugar.

Many diabetics will eat cheese instead of dessert, but fruit desserts (without added sugar) are usually suitable (e.g. fruit salad, baked bananas, fruit fools).

VEGETARIAN

Vegetarians don't eat anything that necessitates the slaughter of animals, e.g. meat. It also includes products derived from animal stomachs, such as lard (used in some pastry), rennet (used in some cheeses), gelatine (used in some wines, jellies etc).

As you are unlikely to have a chalet full of vegetarians, the following recipes serve 1 or 2 as stated.

CHICK PEA TAGINE

Serves 2
1 tbsp olive oil
1 onion, thinly sliced
2 garlic cloves, crushed or finely chopped
2 tsp harissa paste (or substitute ½ tsp chilli powder with ½ tsp ground cumin)
50g dried apricots, roughly chopped
2 large carrots, peeled and thickly sliced
1 red pepper, cored, deseeded and roughly chopped
400ml boiling vegetable stock
1 tbsp tomato puree
410g can chickpeas, drained
salt and freshly ground black pepper

Heat the oil in a large saucepan, add the onion and cook for 5 minutes or until beginning to soften. Add the garlic and harissa and cook for a further minute.
Add the apricots, tomato puree and all the vegetables to the pan and stir. Pour over the stock and bring to the boil. Season to taste, cover and simmer for 15 minutes.
Add the chickpeas and cook for a further 10 minutes or until the vegetables are just tender.
Thicken with a little slaked cornflour if necessary.

MUSHROOM RAGOUT

Serves 2
200g button mushrooms
handful dried mushrooms, soaked and rinsed, boiled 10 mins and drained
4 small shallots
25g butter
1 tbsp oil
2 glass white wine
crème fraîche
salt and freshly ground black pepper

Melt butter and oil in a heavy based pan, add onions and fry gently until soft. Add mushrooms, wine and salt and pepper. **Cook for a few minutes**. Turn the heat up high and reduce liquid down. Add crème fraîche, heat through and serve.

STUFFED PEPPER

Peppers and large tomatoes can be stuffed with all sorts of concoctions. In addition to this recipe, try couscous with cheese and olives, or savoury rice.

Serves 1

1 large pepper
1 tbsp olive oil
½ onion, finely chopped
10g pine nuts
15g breadcrumbs
1 clove garlic, crushed
10g black olives, pitted and finely chopped
1 tbsp chopped parsley
10g grated emmental
salt & pepper

Slice the top off the pepper and keep the lid; scrape out and discard the seeds.

Heat the oil in a pan and fry the onions and garlic until soft. Stir in the pine nuts and breadcrumbs and fry, stirring all the time, until the nuts and crumbs are toasted.

Remove from the heat and stir in the olives, cheese and parsley. Season well.

Stuff pepper with mix, replace lid, cook for about **30 mins. at 180C.**

MELANZANE

Serves 2

1 clove garlic, crushed
½ small onion, finely chopped
2 tbsp olive oil
400g tin chopped tomatoes
1 tbsp tomato puree
10 basil leaves, torn
OR USE JAR OF PASTA SAUCE !

1 aubergine, cut into long slices about 1 cm thick
100g mozzarella, sliced
30g parmesan, grated
salt & pepper

To make your own sauce, fry the onion and garlic gently in half of the oil in a saucepan.

Add the tomatoes and puree and simmer for 15 mins. until thickened. Stir in the basil and season.

Meanwhile, brush the aubergine slices with oil, season and fry until tender.

Spoon a little sauce into the bottom of an ovenproof dish. Cover with a layer of aubergine and mozzarella then repeat, ending with a thin layer of sauce (probably 3-4 layers).

Sprinkle with Parmesan and bake for about **20 minutes at 180C** until bubbling and golden.

ROASTED PEPPERS WITH BEANS AND GOATS' CHEESE

Serves 2
2 red peppers, halved through the stalk, deseeded
400g can cannellini or flageolet beans, drained and rinsed
100g firm goats' cheese, sliced
4 tsp pesto
olive oil

Place the pepper halves in a small roasting tin and divide the beans between them. Drizzle with olive oil, cover with the cheese slices and top with pesto.
Cover with foil and bake at **200C for 20 minutes**, or until peppers are softening. Remove foil and bake for another **10 minutes**.

LENTIL ROAST

Serves 1
200g drained tinned puy lentils
2 tbsp of breadcrumbs
1 tbsp tomato puree
½ clove garlic, crushed
½ tsp thyme
1 egg, beaten
salt and pepper

Place the drained lentils in a bowl and add the bread crumbs, tomato puree, garlic and herbs. Mix well with a fork, mashing the lentils slightly, season with salt and pepper.
Add enough egg to bind the mixture together.
Oil a large ramekin, coffee cup or clean empty tin (making sure the vessel is oven proof). If you are making this for more people then use a loaf tin lined with baking parchment.
Pour the mixture into the ramekin (or other) and bake at **180C for 20 minutes (small containers) or 30 minutes for a loaf tin.** After this time the mixture will have risen, be firm to the touch and slightly browned on top. Turn out straight away.

ASPARAGUS AND RED PEPPER FILO PARCELS

Serves 1
2 circles filo pastry
¼ red pepper, sliced
3-4 shoots green asparagus (from a jar)
1 tbsp crème fraiche
black pepper

Layer the filo circles onto a lined baking tray, brushing each lightly with sunflower oil.
Fill with pepper and asparagus
Add crème fraiche and black pepper
Scrunch the tops of the pastry together and tie with string
Bake for 10 minutes at 200C until golden brown
Remove string before serving.

SURPRISE DE LEGUMES

Serves 2
about 200g chopped assorted vegetables e.g.carrots, leeks, courgettes, mangetout, sweetcorn, green beans, peppers
1 clove garlic, crushed
sunflower oil

For sauce:
15g butter
1 tbsp flour
300ml milk
2 tsp tomato puree
salt & pepper

For topping:
70g breadcrumbs
30g grated cheese

Stir fry vegetables with garlic in a little oil for about 5 minutes; place in a baking dish.
Make a roux sauce (see Techniques earlier); whisk in tomato puree; pour over vegetables
Mix the breadcrumbs with the cheese; sprinkle over the vegetable/sauce mix and bake for about **20 minutes at 200C** until golden brown.

CHILLI BEANS

Serves 2-3
1 onion, chopped
1 red/green chilli and 1 pepper, deseeded and chopped
1 clove garlic, crushed
100g mushrooms
1 tin chopped tomatoes
400g tin kidney beans
1 tbsp oil?
½ tsp chilli powder

Fry onion in oil till soft; add peppers, chilli, mushrooms and garlic and cook till soft.
Add chilli powder, cook 1 minute.
Add tomatoes, simmer 10 minutes.
Add beans, simmer 10 minutes.
Thicken with cornflour slaked with water if required.

Serve with boiled rice and tortilla chips.

CREAM CHEESE & ROASTED RED PEPPER PARCELS

Serves 1
1 red pepper
75g cream cheese
flaky pastry
beaten egg

Cut the pepper into quarters; remove the core and seeds and roast, skin side up, in a hot oven for 10-15 minutes until the pepper is soft and the skin charred. Allow to cool slightly then remove the skin.

Cut the pastry so that you have a piece large enough to form a parcel around 2 pieces of pepper.

Place one piece of pepper on the pastry, put half of the cream cheese on the pepper, then another piece of pepper on top. Fold the pastry around the contents then use the egg wash to stick down the joins and to glaze the top. Repeat to make a second parcel.

Place the parcels on a greased baking tray then cook at **200C for about 10 minutes** until crispy and golden brown.

CHICK PEA PATTIES WITH RAITA

Serves 2
1 small onion, chopped:
1 garlic clove: chopped:
1 tsp cumin:
1 tsp ground coriander:
grated zest of 1 lemon:
25g fresh breadcrumbs:
1 x 410g can chickpeas drained & rinsed:
2 tbsp fresh coriander or parsley, chopped or ½ tsp dried:
1 tbsp olive oil.

It is better to prepare the falafel (patty) mix in the morning as the patties are easier to fry if the mixture has been chilled first.

Blend all ingredients except oil until it comes together as a rough paste, then chill in the fridge for the day if possible.

Shape the mixture into 8 patties. Heat the oil in a frying pan until really hot then add the patties, reduce the heat slightly and fry for a couple of minutes each side. If you prefer just sear them each side in the pan then transfer to a hot oven (about 180C) for about 15 minutes to finish off and keep warm.

Raita:
125g plain yoghurt,
¼ cucumber peeled & coarsely grated,
1 scant tbsp fresh mint, chopped,
1 pinch of cumin seeds,
¼ tsp salt,
1 pinch of Cayenne pepper,
freshly ground black pepper

This is also best made in advance and left in the fridge for the flavours to develop. Mix all the ingredients together, cover and refrigerate.

HAZELNUT ROAST

Serves 2-3
150 g hazelnuts, coarsely chopped
100 g breadcrumbs
1 onion, chopped
1 carrot, grated
salt and pepper
½ tsp mixed herbs
1 egg yolk
 milk

Mix nuts, breadcrumbs, onion, carrots, seasoning and herbs.
Add egg yolk and enough milk to bind mixture.
Place in well greased loaf tin and **bake 45 minutes at 190C.**

VEGETABLE TART TATIN

Serves 4
1 medium aubergine
1 large courgette
1 red onion
1 red pepper
4 tbsp olive oil
1 tsp dried rosemary (or 1 sprig if fresh)
1 tbsp lemon juice
4 cloves garlic, thinly sliced
1 tsp sugar
200g feta cheese, crumbled
50g pine nuts
1 round (375g) puff pastry
salt and pepper
4 sprigs rosemary or parsley, as garnish

Cut aubergine, courgette, pepper and onion into large chunks, place in roasting tin & drizzle with oil; top with rosemary, cover with tin foil, **roast for 25 minutes at 200C.**
Mix in garlic, lemon juice & season to taste. Separate the juice.
Line a baking tin (big enough for 4 people), sprinkle with sugar, then pile in the vegetables, top with feta and pine nuts.
Cover with pastry.
Bake for 35 minutes at 200C, at the bottom of the oven; pastry should be golden brown; allow to rest for a few minutes.
Reduce the juices down to a syrup.
Place a large plate on top of the cooked pastry dish and invert carefully leaving the vegetable mix on top of the pastry.
Drizzle with syrup, garnish & serve immediately.
(Alternatively, make individual servings using small (~18cm) baking trays (or make from tin foil) & divide the pastry into 4 pieces.)

KIDS

Children are often very conservative in their eating habits; even if the parents tell you that the little angels will eat absolutely anything, you may well find that means 'anything they get at home.' So don't be too disappointed if your cottage pie is not the same as mum's.

It is always a good idea to check with the parents at the start of the week, to try and provide food that will be eaten. Then it is up to the parents to get their kids to eat; your job ends with putting the food on the table! Some of the adult food is also suitable for children (e.g. chocolate mousse, cheesecake). And some of the kiddies food is great for chalet hosts!

FISH PIE

serves 3-4
300 g fish (mainly white, but can also include salmon, smoked fish or prawns)
75ml water
75ml milk
1 slice lemon
1 bay leaf
25g butter
25g flour
400g mashed potato

Poach the fish in milk and water with a bay leaf and a slice of lemon in a pan for about 10 minutes; remove skins and flake the fish into a dish.
Melt butter, stir in flour and make a roux; add poaching stock to make sauce (see hints and tips); season to taste.
Pour over fish, cover with mash and dot with butter.
Bake **20-30 minutes at 190C.**

Optional: add cheese/parsley to the sauce

CHICKEN GOUJONS

Cut chicken breasts into small fillets (about 1x3 inches).
Dip into melted butter followed by crushed crisps.
Bake at **190C for about 20 minutes.**

BEEF BURGERS

Serves 2
100g minced beef
½ onion, finely chopped (optional)
a handful of breadcrumbs
2 tsp tomato puree
egg yolk
salt and pepper
sunflower oil for frying

Mix the ingredients together, adding enough egg and breadcrumbs to make it all stick together
Fry in a little oil until well-cooked, about 5 mins per side.

NIKKI'S MASH MOUNTAINS

Pile mashed potato onto a greased baking sheet in the shape of a mountain; sprinkle with grated cheese; bake for about **10mins at 200C**.

POTATO WEDGES

Cut potatoes into about 6 wedges, coat in sunflower oil and roast at **190C for 30-40 minutes**.

SWEET AND SOUR CHICKEN

Serves 4
250g diced chicken
1 tbsp oil
1 onion and 1 pepper, chopped
1 carrot, in matchsticks
½ tin pineapple pieces
2 tbsp demerara sugar
1 tbsp soy sauce
3 tbsp vinegar
1 tbsp tomato puree
150ml water
½ tbsp cornflour

Stir fry the chicken pieces in oil until just starting to brown. Add carrot, onion and pepper, continue frying for 5 minutes.
Add pineapple, sugar, soy sauce, vinegar and tomato puree, cook 1-2 minutes.
Add water, bring to boil.
Mix cornflour with cold water, add to pan , **simmer 5 mins.**
Serve with boiled rice or noodles.

SPAGHETTI CARBONARA

Serves 4
400g spaghetti
1 tbsp olive oil
200g lardons
2 garlic cloves, crushed
2 eggs plus extra yolk or two, mixed together
70 ml double cream
50g grated parmesan, plus extra to serve
salt and pepper

Cook the spaghetti in boiling water for about 10 minutes.
Meanwhile, fry the lardons for about 5 minutes, add garlic and fry for a further minute.
Mix eggs with cream, cheese and seasoning.
Drain spaghetti. Tip back into the hot saucepan off the heat.
Pour egg mixture over pasta, followed by hot lardon mixture.
Toss quickly until it has thickened to a smooth, creamy sauce.
Serve with extra cheese and freshly ground pepper.

PIZZA

Fry a small onion till soft, add tinned tomatoes, tomato puree and oregano/mixed herbs; simmer till thick.
Spread onto prepared pizza bases and cover with ham, mushrooms, peppers, olives (children like to help with this).
Top with mozzarella, grated emmental and parmesan.
Bake about **10-15 mins at 200C.**

COTTAGE PIE

Serves 3-4
300g minced beef
1 onion, finely chopped
1 clove garlic, crushed
50g plain flour
200 ml beef stock
1 tbsp tomato puree or ketchup
1 tbsp oil
400g mashed potato
25g butter

Fry the onion gently in oil for a few minutes; add garlic and mince and fry until the mince is coloured. Stir in the flour, add tomato puree and slowly add hot stock until the meat is just covered. Simmer for 30 minutes.
Place meat in a shallow dish, cover with mash and dot with butter.
Bake **20 minutes at 200C.**

SPAGHETTI BOLOGNAISE

Serves 3-4
300g minced beef
50g lardons (optional)
1 onion, finely chopped
1 clove garlic, crushed
25g plain flour
1 x 400g tin chopped tomatoes
200 ml red wine or beef stock
2 tbsp tomato puree or ketchup
1 tsp mixed dried herbs
1 bay leaf
1 tbsp oil
300g spaghetti, cooked in boiling salted water for about 10 minutes.

Fry the onion gently in oil for a few minutes; add garlic, mince and lardons; fry until the mince is coloured. Stir in the flour, add tomato puree, herbs and tinned tomatoes and slowly add wine or stock until the meat is just covered. Simmer for 30 minutes.
Serve with grated parmesan.

MACARONI CHEESE

Serves 2

120g macaroni (or penne), cooked according to instructions on packet
50g butter
40g plain flour
400ml milk
150g grated cheddar (or 50g parmesan with 100g emmental/gruyere)
salt and pepper

Melt the butter, stir in the flour and cook for a minute; add the milk a little at a time, stirring to make a smooth sauce. Add half the cheese; season to taste.
Stir in the cooked pasta; place in a shallow dish, sprinkle with the rest of the cheese; bake for **20 minutes at 200C**.

PORK SCHNITZEL

Serves 2

This is a useful recipe to use if you have a large joint of pork for the adults. Simply cut slices off the ends for the kids. Alternatively, you can use turkey or chicken breasts.

2 thin pork steaks
1 tbsp plain flour
1 egg, beaten
75g breadcrumbs
1 tbsp sunflower oil
salt and pepper

Place each steak in a plastic back and use a rolling pin to roll it as thin as possible (aim for about half a centimetre). Pat dry with kitchen paper. Dip in flour, then beaten egg, then breadcrumbs.
Heat the oil in a frying pan, then fry the steaks for 2-3 minutes each side.

PASTA WITH PESTO AND PARMESAN

Cook pasta according to instructions on packet; stir in pesto and sprinkle with grated parmesan.

SPAGHETTI WITH MARMITE

Melt a teaspoon of marmite with 50g butter and about a tablespoon of the pasta cooking water. Toss in cooked spaghetti; serve with parmesan.

SPAGHETTI WITH SPICY SARDINES

Mash tinned sardines with their oil, a clove of garlic, a pinch of chilli powder, 2-3 anchovy fillets and some chopped parsley. Add lemon juice to loosen the mixture and stir into cooked spaghetti.

Kids Desserts

Ice cream sundaes (raspberry and meringue; chocolate and nuts)

Banana split (banana, chocolate sauce and icecream)

Fruit and marshmallows with choc sauce dip

Yoghurts

Fruit jelly

Fruit salad (chopped apples, bananas, oranges etc in orange juice)

Chocolate mousse

Crepes (try with lemon and sugar, nutella, banana, ice cream and choc sauce)

Waffles with fruit

Some of the adult desserts are also suitable for children (lemon posset, chocolate pots....)

CHEESEBOARD

If you serve a cheeseboard, try to make it attractive and interesting. Vary the cheeses that you offer and use some kind of garnish if possible. Port is always popular with cheese if your budget allows.

Serve one soft, one hard and one blue cheese each night. Remove the wrapping from cheeses, but leave on rinds. Bring cheeses to room temperature for optimal flavour – take out of the refrigerator up to two hours before serving.

Guests are often interested in what cheeses you are serving but don't worry if you're not an expert just hold onto the wrappings and refer to the notes below.

Garnishes

Dates and walnut halves
Apple and celery
Grapes
Tomato cut into a sunburst
Olives
Gherkins

Soft Cheeses

Brie

Brie is an ancient type of cheese made from pasteurized cow's milk in an area near Paris. It is a sweet, soft cheese, which softens as it ripens. It goes very well with champagne!

Camembert

Camembert is named after a Norman village and it is made from pasteurized cow's milk. At the beginning of its ripening, Camembert is crumbly and soft and gets creamier over time. It is a perfect partner for fresh baguette.

Boursin

This triple-cream cheese is made with cow's milk and cream and flavoured with herbs, garlic or pepper. Boursin goes well with bread, and it is also used to add flavour to many recipes. You can use it in mashed potato or in sandwiches instead of butter, or even in soup instead of sour cream.

Reblochon

Made from full cream milk, Reblochon is ivory in colour with a velvety texture and a subtle, nutty flavour with a strong aroma; it is probably best known for being the classic ingredient of Tartiflette. It becomes bitter when too ripe. The name Reblochon comes from reblochaient, or re-milking. In the Middle-Ages, farmers in the mountains of Haute Savoie used to pay their taxes with part of their milk production. They did not fully milk their cows so as to lower their level of production. Once the tax officers came to measure the milk produced and left, the farmers went back to milk the cows again. The milk they got was much richer and was used to make Reblochon!

Chèvre

Chèvre in French simply means goat. Chèvre cheeses come in a variety of sizes and shapes and are often covered with ash or leaves, herbs or pepper. When young, Chèvre is mild and creamy. When older, the cheese is dry and firm with a slightly sharp and lightly acidic flavor.

Hard Cheeses

Comté

Comté is made from cow's milk in the Jura plateau; it has an ivory colour with small holes and has a nutty, caramelized flavour. Comté is perfect cut into small cubes as an appetizer; it is a traditional fondue cheese and it can also be grated, chunked or melted.

Tomme

"Tomme" is a generic term and means in French 'a wheel of cheese'. Tomme is followed by the name of the village or the region where it is made as in "Tomme de Savoie". Because the cheese is usually made with skimmed milk, Tomme is low in fat content. The rind is thick and grey; legend has it that the rind should never be eaten in case rats have peed on it while it was maturing in the cellars!

Abondance

Abondance cheese (as well as the breed of cow!) is named after the village in Haute Savoie where it originated. It is made from unpasteurised cows' milk and has a soft, creamy texture with a slightly bitter but fruity flavour.

Beaufort

Beaufort cheese is made from cows' milk and comes in three varieties, according to where the cows were kept at the time of milking.

Beaufort d'hiver is a very pale cheese made from winter milk, when the cows are kept indoors.
Beaufort d'été is an aromatic yellow cheese made from milk of cows who are up in mountain pastures during the summer.
Beaufort d'Alpage is made with milk from Tarine (or Tarentaise) cows. They live in the mountains and graze exclusively on natural pastures. This is the tastiest type of Beaufort.

Emmental

Emmental is known as the classic Swiss cheese, first made at Emme in Switzerland and famous for its holes which are formed by the gas produced by a special culture of bacteria. It is also known as 'mouse cheese' after being depicted in numerous 'Tom and Jerry' cartoons. Emmental de Savoie has been made in France since the beginning of the 19th century; it is a traditional, unpasteurized, hard cheese made from cow's milk. It is widely available in French supermarkets, often sold ready grated, and is the cheapest hard cheese. It has mild flavour and a slightly rubbery texture.

Gruyere

Gruyere is named after a Swiss village, and is made from unpasteurized cows' milk. The cheese is slightly grainy, and much tastier than emmental.

Blue Cheeses

Roquefort

Roquefort is a creamy, soft blue cheese made with the milk from specially bred ewes and ripened in limestone caverns under the village of Roquefort-sur-Soulzon. It is slightly crumbly with a tingly, pungent taste. Sometimes called 'the king of cheeses'.

Bleu d'auvergne

Bleu d'Auvergne is a traditional, moist, creamy cheese made from cows' milk. It is delicious in salads with nuts or raw mushrooms. It can be also used as a seasoning for pasta.

Bleu des causses

Bleu des Causses is made from cows' milk and matured for 3 to 6 weeks in the natural caves of the Gorges du Tarn. These caves are exposed to the north and are ventilated by "fleurines", natural chimneys, formed in the cliffs. It is these "fleurines" that allow the cheese to blossom and develop the aroma of the region. The cheese is soft and savoury.

WINE

You'll almost certainly serve wine with your evening chalet dinner. It's normally provided by the Ski Company as a house red and a house white, and sometimes a rosé, so there's no point in discussing here the merits of a Merlot over a Beaujolais. Similarly, whether to serve white with fish and red with meat is irrelevant, you simply serve both every night.

Red wine is served at room temperature or just below, so remember to bring it into the kitchen from any cold store room in plenty of time – at least half-a-day. Wine buffs often recommend that you uncork it an hour or so before dinner, but opinion varies as to the necessity of this. If you're desperate, you can pop a cold bottle into a bowl of warm water; alternatively, put it n the microwave and give it 30-second blasts on low/medium power to warm it up BUT you must remove all foils etc, and of course it's no good for metal screw-caps. Purists will hate you for it so don't show the guests!

White & rosé wine is served chilled. That doesn't mean freezing! Fridge temperature is normally about right.

Some people prefer to see house wine in carafes; personally I think there's nothing wrong with bottles, after all you shouldn't be ashamed of it and it's probably from a local vineyard that might prompt discussion. However, boxed wine definitely needs a carafe.

Wine and beer production often involves the use of animal products, such as gelatine and isinglass, in the *finings* process to clear the fermentation sediment. Vegetarian wines are marketed but it's unlikely that your chalet wine will be one. So you have a ready-made test of your guests' vegetarian principles – confiscate their wine!

Wine is normally served only during dinner up until coffee. I challenge you to deny a guest a quick one just before dinner, or to hide all the bottles as soon as the coffee cups hit the table. Be sensible. Wine is cheap. It can buy you many favours! We sometimes leave out a couple of bottles on our day off but we'd never leave our entire stock within the guests' reach – one group drank our entire supply in one night and then raided the port, and then started on our sister chalet downstairs! Talk about taking the piss!

Whilst on the subject of alcohol, chalets are subject to licensing laws. The rules do vary from country to country and even within regions of a country. For instance, in France: wine with dinner – within reason – is acceptable; beers and spirits should not be sold in the chalet; alcohol brought by guests strictly speaking should not be consumed in the public areas of the chalet, e.g. the living room. In practise, the authorities usually turn a blind eye to casual beer sales from an honesty bar but can be harsh about spirits. Your company should give you guidelines.

CHRISTMAS COOKING MADE EASY

As with everything else in a chalet, organisation and advance preparation are the keys to a successful Xmas dinner. It may seem a bit daunting, especially if you have never cooked a Xmas dinner before, but don't get stressed about it. You will have to think carefully about how to fit everything into your oven….just be prepared! It is definitely worth working out a timing schedule for Xmas dinner.

This is one meal where I would definitely 'family serve' the veg (i.e. place all veg in **warm** dishes on the table, for guests to help themselves); otherwise, by the time you plate up all the meals, the first ones will be cold. We take tinfoil dishes with us just for Xmas & oven cook the veg etc in them and dispose of afterwards – saves masses of washing up time!

Personally I prefer to serve an aperitif with canapés, and omit the starter for Xmas dinner, but if I were expected to provide a starter, I would choose something cold and traditional, such as melon with Parma ham, or a smoked salmon salad.

You really need to be able to get out on the mountain on Xmas day, particularly to avoid possible homesickness; if you spend the day like Cinderella in the kitchen you are likely to end up feeling very sorry for yourself!

Tackling the Turkey

Your company may provide a whole turkey, a turkey crown or a turkey roll for Xmas dinner. A crown is a good compromise; tasty, easy to cook and carve. A whole bird does look more impressive but may be difficult to fit in the oven. Turkey rolls can be very disappointing unless they are top quality. If you are responsible for ordering your own, do so well in advance from the butcher, making sure that it will fit in your oven! A 10lb (4.5 kg) turkey will feed about 12 people.

Try to prepare the turkey, make the stuffing and peel the vegetables on Christmas eve, but do make sure you keep it all chilled. The vegetarian loaf can also be made in advance and reheated. If your turkey is frozen, allow plenty of time to defrost (at least 24 hours in a cool room).

Make sure you remove any giblets from inside the turkey; you can stew them in water with an onion and some seasoning for about an hour to make delicious stock for the gravy.

Stuffing

It's not essential, but it is traditional, tasty and makes the meat go further. If you have a whole bird, it will help to keep the breast meat moist. If you have a crown or roll, the stuffing can be cooked separately.

APPLE AND APRICOT STUFFING

Sufficient for a 5 kg turkey
50g dried apricots, finely chopped
1 tbsp boiling water
50g streaky bacon, finely chopped
1 onion, peeled and finely chopped
2 sticks celery, finely chopped
2 apples, peeled, cored and finely chopped
salt and pepper
75g fresh breadcrumbs
1 egg yolk

Put the apricots in a bowl, cover with boiling water and soak for a couple of hours; drain well.
Fry the bacon in oil until brown; add to apricots.
Fry onion and celery for 2-3 minutes; add apple and fry for another 2-3 minutes; add to bowl with breadcrumbs, seasoning and egg yolk. Add a little lemon juice if necessary to make a stiff paste.

Cooking the turkey

Place the stuffing in the breast end; place a peeled potato and onion in the body cavity, to keep the meat moist and add flavour. Rub about 100g butter all over the breast, season and cover with streaky bacon (optional).

Timings are given for a 4.5 kg turkey which will serve 8 generously; larger birds will take longer.

Cover loosely with foil; place in a hot, preheated oven (220C) for 30 minutes; reduce the heat to 170C and cook for about 2 hours; remove the foil, baste well and increase the heat to 200C for a final 30 minutes until the bird is bronzed and beautiful! Test with a meat thermometer (80C) or insert a skewer into the thickest part of the thigh; the juices should run clear without a hint of pink. It is very important that the turkey is cooked through; better to serve dinner a bit late than risk giving your guests food poisoning.

Allow the turkey to rest, lightly covered with foil, for at least half an hour before carving (this makes it much easier to carve).

Make gravy by stirring a couple of tablespoons of flour into the cooking pan. Cook for a few minutes on the hob, then slowly add stock to make delicious gravy.

Carving the turkey

Carve the turkey at the table if you are confident, or ask the alpha male guest if he would like to carve. If not, carve and plate up the meat in the kitchen, giving everyone a mix of brown and white meat and stuffing. A well carved turkey will give you larger slices and less meat is wasted if you carve the bird properly, so follow the instructions below. You can remove the stuffing either before or after you have carved.

Place the turkey securely on a large carving plate or board. Have a warm serving plate ready so you can transfer the meat with the knife blade as you slice it. To start with, you will be carving only one side of the bird so use a large fork in the breast for balance. Slice down where a leg connects with the body until you reach the bone. Pull the leg away from the body with one hand. With the other, force the edge of the knife into the joint of the leg and body and cut firmly to separate the leg from the body.

Holding the leg up by the small end, rest the large end on the carving board. First carve slices off of the thigh, and then the drumstick parts of the leg. Cut downwards and try to get medium-thin slices, as large as possible. Work your way around the leg.

Next use the fork to pull a wing aside. Insert the point of the knife into the joint and separate the wing from the body. Cut through the joint if necessary and put the wing aside (can be used for stock or soup later). Some people like to remove the wishbone at this stage, to make carving easier.

Now you are ready to carve the breast. Using the large fork for balance, first cut a slice from the most rounded area of the breast (about halfway down).Continue to slice downwards in order to get medium-thin sliccs that gradually become larger until you expose the bones when the slices may become a bit mis-shapen. Don't worry; they still taste good, and you can probably hide them under some better slices.

BREAD SAUCE

100g fresh white breadcrumbs
6 cloves
1 bayleaf
8 black peppercorns
500ml milk
50g butter
2 tbsp cream
salt and pepper

Cut the onion in half and stick the cloves in it; place it in a saucepan with the bay leaf, peppercorns, salt and milk. Bring to the boil, then remove from the heat, cover the pan and leave in a warm place for the milk to infuse for two hours or more.
When you're ready to make the sauce, remove the onion, bay leaf and peppercorns. Stir the breadcrumbs into the milk and add 1 oz (25 g) of the butter. Leave the saucepan on a very low heat, stirring now and then, until the crumbs have swollen and thickened the sauce – about 15 minutes. Stir in the remaining butter and the cream and taste to check the seasoning. Serve in a warm jug.

Roast potatoes and parsnips
Part boil the peeled potatoes for about 10 minutes if you want to cut down roasting time. Then drain, shake well in the empty pan and tip into a roasting tin that has been preheated with some vegetable oil or lard. Baste all the potatoes with the oil and roast for about an hour at 200C. I like to turn and baste the potatoes halfway through roasting.
Parsnips do not take as long as potatoes and do not need boiling first. Peel, cut lengthwise into quarters and roast for about 40 minutes at 200C.

Pigs in blankets
Wrap cocktail sausages in slices of bacon. Cook for about 20 minutes at 200C.

Sprouts
Even at altitude, sprouts don't take long to cook; overcooked sprouts are vile.
Remove outer leaves; cook in boiling salted water for about 15 minutes.
Can be served sprinkled with flaked almonds.

Vegetarian fruit and nut loaf

Serves 2-3
2 onions, finely chopped
1tbsp olive oil
2 cloves garlic, finely chopped
handful thyme leaves
120g mushrooms (preferably chestnut or shitake), chopped
1 glass red wine
250g stoned prunes, chopped
300g mixed nuts (hazelnuts, chestnuts, pistachio…), finely chopped
2 apples, peeled, cored and chopped
2 eggs
salt and pepper

In a large frying pan, heat the oil then add onion and a pinch of salt. Cook gently until soft, add garlic and thyme, cook for 2 minutes; add mushrooms and cook for a further 5 minutes. Raise heat and add wine. Let it bubble, then simmer gently for about 5 minutes. Remove from heat and set aside to cool.
Add nuts, prunes, apple and enough egg to bind. Season with salt and pepper and spoon into loaf tin, then sit this in a roasting tin and fill up with hot water to half way up sides, cover with foil and put in oven and cook for about 20-30 minutes at 190C. Remove foil and cook for a further 10 mins, till golden and cooked through. Allow to cool slightly, then remove from tin and slice. Garnish with rosemary or thyme sprigs.

Christmas pudding

You will probably be provided with a pudding. Follow the manufacturer's recommendations for heating, but as a guide you will probably need to steam it for about an hour. It is possible to heat a pudding in the microwave, but be very careful as the high sugar content might cause it to catch fire; allow it to rest between successive short bursts of power (probably about 30 minutes in total; don't be tempted to omit the rest periods). The recipe below is a tasty alternative to a traditional pud, and can be made at the last minute.

Speedy Christmas Pudding

150g cranberry sauce, mixed with 3tbsp golden syrup
150g soft butter
150g soft brown sugar
3 eggs, beaten
150g plain flour
2 tbsp mixed ground spice
450g dried mixed fruit
2 apples, peeled, cored and grated

Grease a large (1.5 litre) pudding basin.
Place half the cranberry mixture in the bottom of the bowl; reserve the rest for serving.
In another bowl, beat all remaining ingredients together and spoon into the prepared bowl.
Cover with baking paper; microwave for about 10 minutes until springy. Alternatively, steam for an hour and a half.
Allow to stand for 10 minutes before turning out onto a warm plate.
Cover with the remaining (warmed) cranberry sauce and serve immediately.

RUM (OR BRANDY) SAUCE

75g butter
60g plain flour
50g cup sugar
500ml milk
3 tbsp rum or brandy
2 tbsp cream

Melt butter in a small saucepan over medium heat. Add the flour to make a roux, then slowly add milk a little at a time, and cook stirring frequently until the mixture begins to boil. Add sugar and continue cooking until thick, stirring constantly. Remove from heat, and stir in rum and cream. Serve warm.

Flaming the pud

Setting the pudding alight is one of the most impressive parts of Xmas dinner. It's quite simple to do, but do make sure you don't set the chalet on fire! It helps if you have an assistant to light the brandy as you pour it over the pudding. The flames don't last long, so make sure you dim the lights and light the brandy where the guests can see the flames!

Tip the pudding out of its bowl onto a **warm** plate. Heat a little (about 50ml) brandy in a small saucepan, but don't let it boil. Light the brandy in the pan and pour over the pudding.

BLACK FOREST TRIFLE

This is a traditional alternative to Xmas pud; make extra plain yoghurt cake a day or two beforehand
About ½ a plain cake
500g frozen forest fruits (or raspberries), defrosted
2 tbsp crème de cassis
500ml cold custard (see below for making your own)
300ml cream, whipped to soft peaks with a dash of vanilla extract

If you are unable to buy custard, it isn't difficult to make your own (and much tastier).
Mix 5 egg yolks, 2 tsp cornflour, a few drops of vanilla and 25g caster sugar in a bowl.
Bring 300ml cream and 300ml milk to the boil in a pan and pour it onto the egg mixture, whisking well.
Rinse out the pan, pour the mix back into the pan and heat gently, whisking all the time, until the custard thickens. Cover closely with clingfilm to prevent a skin forming and cool before assembling the trifle.

Arrange half the cake and fruit in the bowl; drizzle with cassis and cover with half the custard. Repeat. Cover with cream. Just before serving, decorate with a few berries, a drizzle of cassis and perhaps a few nuts (chopped pistachios look good).

MINCE PIES

Mince pies can be assembled in advance, kept in the fridge and cooked when required.

Shortcrust pastry
Mincemeat (add a tbsp of brandy, grated orange rind and/or a grated apple for extra flavour)

Cut out circles of pastry and line patty tins.
Place a heaped teaspoon of mincemeat in each; cover with a smaller circle or a star of pastry.
Bake at 200C for about 20 minutes until golden. Remove from tins before any escaped mincemeat sets into sticky toffee and cool on a wire rack. Dredge with icing or caster sugar to serve.

Ginger Snaps

This is a good recipe for cut-out shapes; e.g. stars. The biscuits can be decorated with icing, silver balls etc.

100g plain flour
pinch salt
2 tsp ground ginger
½ tsp raising agent
100g caster sugar
75g butter
2 tbsp golden syrup

Melt butter and syrup, add to dry ingredients, roll out thinly and cut out into shapes.
Bake 10-12 mins at 170 C.
Cool on wire rack before decorating or eating!

Last-minute Christmas cake

500g mixed dried fruit e.g. sultanas, raisins, currants
100g ready to eat apricots, chopped
100g dates, chopped
50g dried cranberries
150g glace cherries, halved
225ml cold black tea, made from two teabags
100ml brandy
75ml orange juice
zest of 1 orange
2 tbsp black treacle
200g butter, softened
200g soft brown sugar
250g plain flour
1 level tsp raising agent
5 eggs, beaten
2 tsp mixed spice
75g chopped nuts

In a large pan mix together the dried fruits, apricots, dates, cranberries and cherries. Add the cooled tea, whisky or brandy, orange juice, zest and treacle. Bring to the boil, stirring. Simmer gently for 10 minutes. Remove from the heat and leave to cool. Transfer to a bowl and chill overnight or as long as you can.
Lightly grease a 20cm round cake tin and line with baking parchment. Wrap the sides of the cake in a double thickness of brown paper or newspaper.
Place all the remaining cake ingredients, except the nuts, into a large mixing bowl. Mix thoroughly, and then fold in the tea-soaked fruit and nuts.
Spoon the mixture into the prepared tin. **Bake at 140C for 3 hours**; check and cover with baking paper if the surface is getting too brown. **Bake for a further 30 minutes-1 hour,** or until a metal skewer inserted into the centre comes out clean.
Cool in the tin for 15 minutes then turn out and allow to cool completely on a wire rack.

Timings for Xmas dinner

Day before (at least!)
Check that you have all ingredients
Defrost turkey
Make stuffing
Prepare mince pies (but don't cook)
Make Xmas biscuits
Make veggie option
Make custard and yoghurt cake for trifle
Prep veg (pots, parsnips, carrots, sprouts)
Prepare a cold canapé (e.g. pepper wraps)
Make breadcrumbs for bread sauce

Xmas morning
Remove giblets
Prep pigs in blankets
Stuff turkey and prepare for cooking
Cook mince pies; leave for afternoon tea
Assemble trifle
Put fizz and white wine in fridge
Infuse milk for bread sauce

time	n.b. assumes dinner is at 8pm	Oven temp C
4.00pm	Turkey in oven	220
4.30	Lower oven temp	170
	shower, chill out……enjoy a mince pie?	
6.00	Make rum sauce Lay table	
6.30	Put potatoes on to boil Increase oven temp; remove foil and baste turkey Make canapés (e.g. blinis)	200
6.45	Start steaming pudding Make bread sauce	
7.00	Drain potatoes, put in roasting tin in oven Start cooking carrots Test turkey; remove from oven when cooked, cover with foil	
7.15	Put parsnips in oven Make gravy Warm plates Open red wine	
7.40	Pigs in blankets in oven Start cooking sprouts Serve aperitif and canapes Carve turkey White wine and water on table	
8.00	Serve dinner	

PRESENTATION

Food presentation is *very* important – it cannot be overemphasised!

No matter how tasty your food is, nobody will be impressed if it is not attractive to look at. It is said that *we firstly eat with our eyes*. Appealing presentation is largely a matter of common sense:

> ➤ Never use chipped or cracked plates.
> ➤ Always wipe drips and smudges off plates.
> ➤ Don't overfill plates (much better to leave some space and offer seconds later).
> ➤ Serve food artistically! For some reason, things always look better in odd numbers, so serving 3 slices of meat will look better than 2.
> ➤ Use garnishes to brighten up the meal (see below).
> ➤ Above all, make it look like you've made an effort and not just "thrown it on the plate"!
> ➤ AND ALWAYS TASTE IT BEFORE YOU SERVE IT.

GARNISHING

A garnish needs to add something to the overall appearance of the dish; usually it provides a contrasting colour or texture. A garnish can be as simple as a sprig of a fresh herb or as complex as an intricately carved vegetable. Don't overdo it; you can have too much of a good thing.

Look at the ingredients you are using and see if there is anything there that you can pick out to use as a garnish. For example if you've used coconut milk in the dish, you could choose to garnish it with toasted coconut flakes

Sometimes you don't need to add a garnish as such, as the individual components within the dish can themselves become the garnish - sauces, vegetables, salads and fruit can all become attractive garnishes.

Sprinkling or Scattering

Small garnishes can be sprinkled or scattered either over the food or sometimes on the plate around the food, such as:

> ➤ Pine nuts sprinkled over a lamb tagine
> ➤ Grated white chocolate scattered over a dark chocolate mousse
> ➤ Raspberry coulis drizzled over the plate around white chocolate cheesecake
> ➤ Sesame seeds sprinkled over noodles
> ➤ Grated parmesan sprinkled on top of spaghetti bolognaise
> ➤ Sour cream swirled into soup
> ➤ Icing sugar sieved over apple pie

Natural garnishes

Food in its natural state, such as a sprig of herbs or a wedge of lemon, makes a lovely garnish. Herbs you also provide the added bonus of their delicious aromas. Try some of the following:

> ➤ Sprig of mint on chocolate torte
> ➤ Basil leaves on tomato salads
> ➤ Lemon wedges with fish
> ➤ Fresh berries on desserts
> ➤ Sprig of rosemary with roast lamb
> ➤ Chives crossed on top of pale coloured casseroles
> ➤ Parsley on scrambled eggs

Artistic garnishes

When you are really out to impress, try some vegetable carving!

Radish flowers

Top and tail radishes and stand upright. Make a series of cuts vertically down about ¾ of the way towards the base. Soak in iced water to open up the flower.

Carrot Curls

Peel and then slice a carrot lengthwise into thin slices with a vegetable peeler. Roll up and fasten with cocktail sticks. Chill in bowl of iced water. Remove sticks before serving. If desired, place sprig of parsley or watercress through each carrot curl.

To make carrot curls to float in a soup or top a casserole, steam the carrots with a tablespoon of water in the microwave for thirty seconds. They'll go limp and be easy to curl and drape on a plate or dish.

Carrot Sticks

Peel carrots and cut into narrow lengthwise strips. Chill in bowl of iced water. If desired, dip ends of chilled carrot sticks into softened cream cheese; sprinkle with snipped parsley.

Celery Curls

Cut stalks of celery into short lengths. Slit both ends into narrow strips almost to centre. To curl ends, chill in iced water.

Cucumber Sails

Run a fork down the length of the cucumber to make deep furrows, then repeat all the way around the cucumber. Cut into very thin slices and each will have a *crinkly* edge. Twist the slice in a loose figure-of-eight shape and place vertically in savoury mousses etc

Tomato sunburst

Use a very sharp knife to cut a zig zag around the tomato, cutting only about half way through. Separate the two halves carefully.

Apple staircase

Cut a small slice off an apple such that it will sit (and not roll) with its stalk visible but slanting downwards. Make 2 cuts to form a small V-shape in the top (exposed) part of the apple. Cut a bigger V-shape to enclose the first. Cut another to enclose both. Slide the 3 pieces of cut apple to make a "staircase". Makes a cheeseboard come alive!

TABLE LAYING

The evening meal should have a dinner party atmosphere, so it is worth spending a little time making the table look attractive. The following suggestions are guidelines:

➤ Jugs of cold water with ice and lemon (put out just before service)
➤ Chilled white wine (keep in fridge & put out just before service)
➤ Red wine at room temperature
➤ Butter (cubed)
➤ Salt and pepper
➤ Bread (cut into slices) in a basket (put out just before service)
➤ Serving spoons, for vegetables, if required
➤ Mats for hot dishes
➤ Candles (nightlights in glass jars are less prone to being knocked over)
➤ Side plates (if you have room on the table)
➤ Glasses for wine and water
  o May need separate glasses for white and rosé wine (generally a straighter glass) and red wine (generally the lip curves inward)
➤ Cutlery for each course, as necessary, with starter cutlery on the outside
  o Always need a butter knife, which may be used for starter also
  o Can put butter knife on side plate
  o Dessert cutlery may not need a fork
  o Desserts like fools, possets etc may be served in a glass, on a saucer with a teaspoon
➤ Napkins (either in the wine glass, or between the knife & fork, or on the side plate)

Sometimes you will plate up the entire meal; at other times you may prefer to plate up meat and 'family serve' the vegetables in large dishes which you place in the middle of the table for guests to serve themselves. When family serving, provide all vegetables at each end of the table so that all guests can easily reach all the vegetables.

Remember to warm all plates that will have hot food served on them: either in a microwave – 6 plates at a time (to prevent overloading the turntable motor) for about 3 minutes (there's no need to add water), or in the dishwasher, or in a sink of hot water (but they'll need drying), or in the oven (but take care not to burn your guests).

It is considered polite to serve the guests from their left hand side using your left hand, and collect their plate afterwards from their right with your right hand, except for drinks which should be served on the right with your right hand.

AFTERNOON TEA

Guests love returning to the chalet for their cake! Afternoon tea is not usually laid out formally like a meal, usually it is stacked on a side-table or similar before you leave the chalet in the morning. But it's still a chance to impress!

You will typically need:

➢ Tea cups & saucers or mugs, and teaspoons
➢ Tea & coffee making facilities, including sugar & milk (normally left in the fridge)
➢ Bread, wrapped in a serviette, and a knife, butter and jams (all covered)
➢ Tea plates & serviettes (maybe interleaved in the plate stack for show)
➢ Butter knives, perhaps arranged artistically
➢ And finally, the cake… in a cake stand or similar, together with a suitable knife; and a label saying what it is and a friendly "*bon appétit*"

NAPKIN FOLDING

Most days you probably won't want to spend time folding napkins to make intricate shapes. My personal favourite involves the time honoured method of opening out the napkin, pinching together at the centre and placing in the glass. However, for times when you really want to impress, and have time to spare, here are a few relatively easy alternatives.

Standing fan
Open napkin once, keeping open long side towards you
Fold accordion style starting at LHS, leaving a couple of inches unfolded
Fold whole in half (bottom to top) keeping the accordion folds on outside
Grasp unfolded top RHS corners, keeping them together, fold diagonally and tuck under the folds to form a support at the back
Open into fan

Goblet fan
Open napkin once
Fold accordion style, starting at a long side
Fold whole in half and place in glass

Twin candle roll
Open napkin and fold in half diagonally
Roll tightly from the long side to the point
Fold in half and place in glass

Bird of paradise
Place unopened napkin with open point down (towards you)
Fold in half (open point up to closed point)
Now fold RH point down so long RH edge points vertically down along centre line
Repeat with LHS
Fold lower points up under the rest
Press lower corners together so that centre rises up, making a sort of boat shape
Hold tightly while you pull up the individual points

See www.ChristmasMagazine.com and www.napkinfoldingguide.com for further details.

Pyramid

Open napkin and fold it in half on the diagonal.

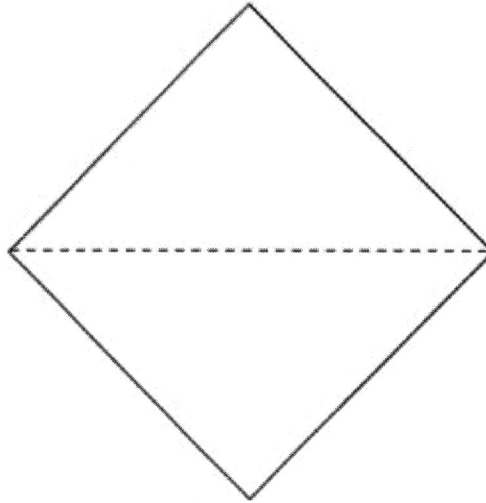

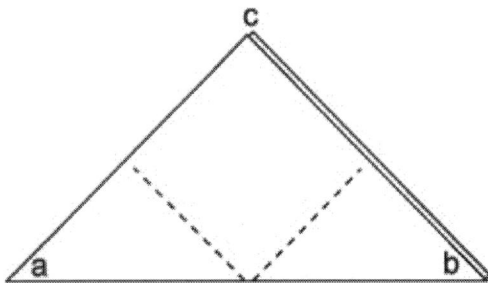

Fold corner a to point c.

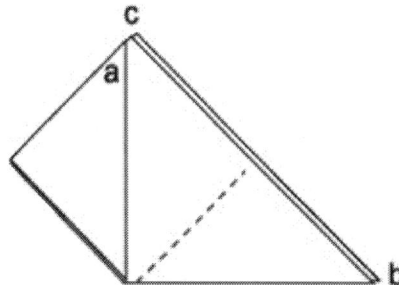

Repeat with corner b.

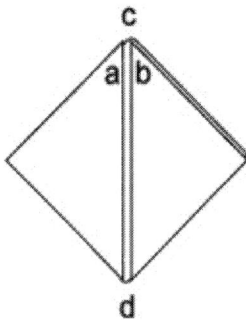

The result is a square.

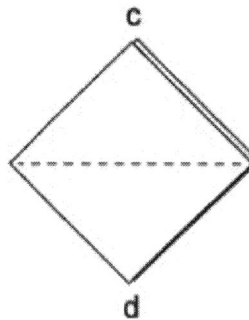

Turn napkin over, keep points c and d at the same position. Fold diagonally in half.

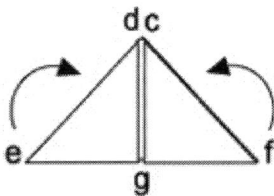

Lift g towards you and at the same time move points e and f closer together.

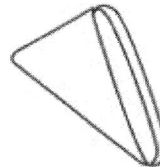

Finished.

Diamond Pocket

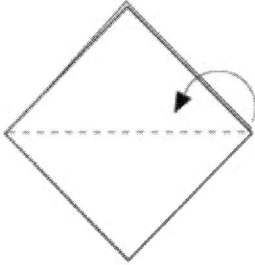

Fold the top layer back to the center and tuck inside so it lays flat and forms a pouch.

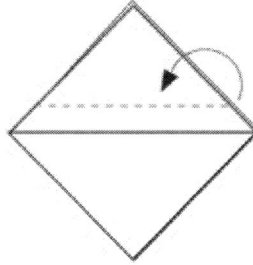

Tuck the second layer inside leaving about an inch exposed.

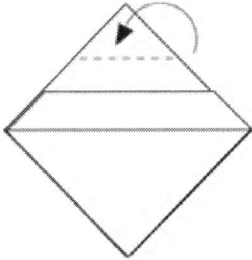

Tuck the third layer inside again leaving about an inch exposed.

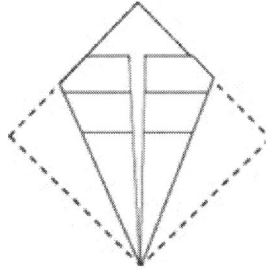

Flip the napkin. Fold the left and the right corner towards the middle.

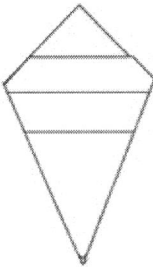

Flip the folded napkin over again. Finished.

Silverware Pocket

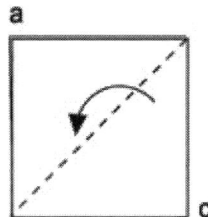

a

c

With the closed side facing right, fold down the top layer from point a to c.

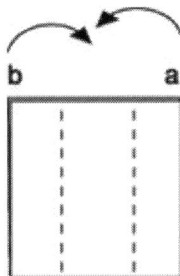

b   a

Flip the napkin over. Fold the left side and then the right side 1/3 towards middle. Tuck the bottom parts together.

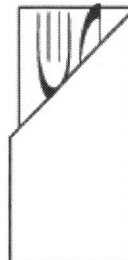

Flip the napkin back with the front side facing up. Slide in the desired cutlery and lay the napkin on a plate.

MONEY MATTERS

Having covered all the food cooking in previous chapters, we could have jokingly entitled this chapter *"Cooking The Books"*! But money is serious and anyone who fiddles the company budget, or abuses any form of trust, will be on the first plane home – at their own expense – and rightly so.

Budgets

All companies work to a budget although you may never actually know what your budget is. Our first company simply told us if we were *on budget* or not.

The budget is company-confidential and should <u>never ever</u> be told to guests. Why? Because it is surprisingly small!
A guest may pay £500-1,000 for a week's holiday and you may be allocated a budget of say £50-100 for his food, i.e. probably less than 10%. But don't worry, whatever the budget is, it will always be enough. The company has no interest in trying to make you fail.

Your budget may include only food, or it may also include cleaning products. It may exclude bread and/or wine, which are often bought in bulk by the company. You may be given extra budget for your own food. Every company is different and they'll explain their method to you.

Budget overspend can theoretically be deducted from your deposit/bond (although this rarely happens in practice) so it's important to keep a tight grip on it. Don't get too upset if you go over budget in the first few weeks, you will inevitably spend more at the beginning of the season when you start with bare cupboards and it may take several weeks before you begin to feel under control. We have pleaded with companies to allocate an extra start-up budget so that you can see you're on track from day one but we know of no one who has implemented this (but everyone says that it'd be a good idea!)

Look out for the cheapest ways of buying your ingredients. Most of the bigger supermarkets show the price per kilo on the shelf ticket. For non-perishables, it is usually more economical to buy large packets, provided that you will use it all during the season. Many own brand products are considerably cheaper than branded goods of similar quality. However some guests may *turn up their nose* at budget packets on the table. We know of chalet hosts who buy *Kellogs* in their first shop and then re-fill the pack with a budget brand – and then curse when a helpful guest screws up the empty box for the bin! Similarly, *Bonne Maman* jam jars look top-quality even when filled with budget jam (with the labels removed, of course)!

Perishable goods are another matter; never buy more than you will use in a week and keep a close eye on sell-by dates.

Minimising waste is the best way of staying within budget. You will get better at this as the season progresses. Try to prevent guests from pinching food from the kitchen (midnight munchies can play havoc with the budget). The guests will be getting great breakfasts and dinners, but lunches and snacks are not usually included in the deal. If possible, keep the bulk of the food in a separate (preferably locked) storeroom, and only take food into the kitchen as you need it.

Top tips:
- keep empty jars and a stock of plastic bags for storing leftover ingredients; use a permanent marker to label them
- where possible, cook large batches of foods, sauces etc and store/freeze in meal-size portions to save time each week, e.g. onions, red cabbage, bolognaise sauce
- use clothes pegs to close food bags once opened to minimise spillage and wastage
- cut butter into 1cm cubes rather than putting a whole 250g pack in a butter dish; it will minimise waste
- serve jam in small jars as a large jar could be spoilt by guests with dirty/contaminated knives

- serve sugar in small pots as guests can contaminate the whole pot with a wet spoon
- serve milk in small jugs for afternoon tea as it will warm up during use and may not be suitable for putting back in the fridge
- buy a small squeezy bottle of honey and re-fill from a large pot
- chop up left over lemons & limes and freeze them, then add to the water jugs on the table
- when you buy parsley treat it like flowers and put it in a jar of water- it will live happily in your kitchen and look pretty
- if you serve pancakes with genuine (expensive!) maple syrup then do it near the end of the week, otherwise guests will want it every day!

Shopping

Ski companies have lots of different methods of organising the shopping. You may have total control over your own shopping, as long as you keep within budget, or at the other extreme you may have your ingredients delivered weekly as a standard order.

Generally speaking, shopping day is not one of a chalet host's favourites! For some bizarre reason, the sun often shines and the snow is great on shopping days. Therefore the best approach is to be organised, get on with it and get it over and done with.

First and foremost, unless you have an amazing memory, you need a list! At the start of each season, we spend time walking round the supermarket, making a list of everything we might ever need, in shop order. Then we print out lists in that order and each week we check our stock and tick off what we need to buy. On the same list we also have the maximum quantity of each item that we'll need each week based on our standard weekly menu. So quite simply the amount to buy that week is the maximum needed less any stock, and then adjust for any known dietary requirements. Even if you don't print out lists, try to make your shopping list in the order you walk around the shop; it saves lots of unnecessary back tracking.

Go through your stock before you make your shopping list, check all sell-by dates and throw away any suspect food. Try to keep some staple foods in reserve; you never know when you will get an unexpected vegetarian or a culinary disaster.

At the end of the book there is a list of common ingredients with their French translations.

Company money

You will often be given a store-card so that no cash is required. But if you do operate with cash then take great care of receipts for items you buy as without the receipt you will probably not get the cash reimbursed.

You will have some form of paperwork to complete each week detailing what you've spent, either with cash or on account. We strongly recommend you keep your own separate records so that if your company queries your finances at any time you have proof of your expenses. One chalet host was erroneously accused of going way over budget by her manager. She had kept a track of her expenses and could prove the manager himself had made an error. Without that record she would possibly be forking out of her own pocket for overspend!

You don't need anything complicated:

Week 1	
Brought forward over/underspend	0.00
Budget for 10 guests @ 50 each	+500.00
Main shop at Carrefour (on account)	-550.00
Bread	-50.00
Local shop (cash) – vegetables	-10.00
Carried forward over/underspend	-110.00
Week 2	
Brought forward over/underspend	-110.00
Budget for 12 guests@ 50 each	+600.00
Main shop at Carrefour (on account)	-490.00
Bread	-50.00
Local shop (cash) – none	0.00
Carried forward over/underspend	-50.00

Personal money

Rule 1 – never mix your own money with company money; use a separate wallet/purse.

Rule 2 – never buy personal stuff with company money, even if you intend paying it back later.

Rule 3 – never carry large amounts of cash; you wouldn't at home & there's simply no need.

You won't need much cash. There's nothing much you need to buy. Just a few occasional beers – OK, so you might need a bit more! Hopefully your tips will cover your casual spending leaving your salary untouched in the bank.

Take out some euros (or relevant currency) with you as there may not be a service till near you. Cash tills abroad work the same as at home but withdrawing cash abroad is expensive as there's usually a transaction fee plus a currency conversion charge. Don't withdraw lots of small amounts – it'll cost you in fees, instead withdraw a reasonable amount but leave most of it hidden in your room, or in a company safe etc. Bear in mind that it's a long time until your first payday so ensure you have enough float to last you.

Many new card products are becoming available that are ideal for working abroad, e.g. FairFX, Caxton. They allow you to pre-load with sterling from your bank a/c via a website, then withdraw currency at ATMs.

Ski resorts are generally very low crime-rate areas but be careful. At bars etc (especially those with road access) either lock your skis or swap one ski with a friend and leave each pair some distance from the other. Bars and clubs in the evening are probably the main place you're likely to get robbed so leave your ski pass back in your room, don't carry lots of cash and keep an eye on your nice new jacket (better still, don't take it – it'll get covered in beer!)

And don't be seduced by flashy new skis or gear (at least not until you've earned the money)!

Tips

Fact 1: never expect a tip.

Fact 2: you'll be disappointed if you don't get one.

It is always lovely to receive tips, especially when you have gone the extra mile and feel you deserve recognition, but don't expect them every week as there are some people who never tip. Sometimes you have an amazing fun week and get nothing, and other times it's the fussy grumpy people who leave a big tip. You just can't tell so don't take offence.

How much? Tips vary from a few euros to a few hundred euros if you are really lucky. If a chalet of ten guests is booked out to a family then you may get say twenty euros – bear in mind it's only the parents who are tipping, whereas if it's booked to five couples you may get five times twenty euros. And in either case you may get *zilch, nada, zero, nuffink* – and after say three weeks of nil tips you do start getting a bit narked!

CLEANING

There are some people who get a kick out of cleaning, but for most of us it is a necessary chore to be completed as efficiently as possible! You will be told what your company expects in the way of cleaning, but here are a few hints and tips.

Try to get into the habit of wearing rubber gloves for all cleaning jobs. Your hands WILL suffer in this job, and if they get really sore and start to crack, they may not recover all season. We always take pre-work barrier cream with us to try and protect our hands as much as possible, particularly on changeover days. Also, products such as *Sudocrem* work for some people as a barrier and/or healer. It's a good idea to take some old lightweight clothes for cleaning (don't be tempted to use bleach in good clothes!)

You will be expected to deep clean your chalet before the first guests arrive. Take pride in this lovely clean state and try to keep as near to it as possible throughout the season. Once you start to let your standards slip, it is hard to get them back up again. At the end of the season you will be expected to deep clean again, so if you let the dirt creep in, you are only storing up work for later! Many companies insist on a mid-season deep clean too.

During each week, the chalet will get messy while your guests are there, but on changeover day you can restore it to its pristine state!

You will probably have to clean the bathrooms, make beds and empty bins on a daily basis. Have a bucket containing all your daily cleaning materials which should contain:
- ➢ Glass cleaning spray
- ➢ Spray cleaner for baths and basins e.g. cif
- ➢ Two differently coloured cloths (e.g. *pink for sinks and blue for loos*)
- ➢ Polishing cloth (old towel or bath mat works well) for buffing mirrors and ceramics
- ➢ Loo cleaner
- ➢ Spare loo rolls
- ➢ Bin liners
- ➢ An old toothbrush for cleaning round taps, sink traps, ventilators, edges of baths etc
- ➢ Rubber gloves

On a daily basis you should consider cleaning the following:
- ➢ Kitchen: surfaces, sink, fridge, floor, bin, cooker, all spillages/stains
- ➢ Dining & living areas: floor, tables, cushions
- ➢ Bedrooms: bins, sinks/baths/showers, mirrors, floors, make beds
- ➢ Other areas (e.g. boot rooms): bins, floor

In some chalets, you'll be expected to keep a log of what was cleaned & when. This is mandatory in Austria and you may find that Austrian chalet owners are very closely involved in the regular cleaning and general upkeep of their chalets.

Hints and tips for speedy, effective cleaning
- ➢ Buff mirrors, baths and sinks with a clean dry cloth after cleaning; it removes water marks and makes them sparkle.
- ➢ Always use special proprietary cleaners for ceramic hobs and marble worktops.
- ➢ Vacuum floors before washing to remove loose dirt, and wash the kitchen floor frequently to avoid sticky residues building up.
- ➢ Make friends with bleach, but take care to avoid splashes as bleach can ruin your clothes and carpets:

- pour down smelly sink traps
- attack mould on bath sealant
- remove tea and coffee stains from sink
- remove red wine stains from stripped pine tables
- clean tea pots etc

➢ Use a paste of bleach mixed with bicarbonate of soda for really stubborn stains.

➢ Dishwasher tablets dissolved in a little warm water are good cleaners, especially for tile grout.

➢ Treat wine stains on fabric by covering with wet salt (or put white wine on a red wine stain); leave for an hour then wash as normal.

➢ Remove blood stains by prolonged soaking in cold water.

➢ To clean wax off candle sticks, wash in very hot water, then dry with paper towel.

➢ Slight burn marks on carpets can sometimes be removed by rubbing vigorously with the cut surface of an onion.

➢ Particularly dirty windows are best cleaned by washing with hot soapy water, rinsing with water containing a little vinegar, and polished with newspaper.

➢ Remove grease & wax spots from curtains, clothes etc by covering with paper towel and pressing with a hot iron. Neat washing up liquid, well rubbed in then sponged off, often works on grease.

➢ Don't use disinfectant to clean the inside of the fridge, as the smell lingers for weeks. Wash with a dilute solution of sodium bicarbonate or raising agent (2 tsp / litre), rinse with clean water, and dry. Wipe the fridge inside and out at least once a week – just before shopping day makes sense as it'll be fairly empty.

➢ Remove chewing gum from carpets or fabric by pressing an ice cube over the gum; it should harden and peel off.

Washing Up

I wouldn't have thought it necessary to include tips on washing up but having seen some students on our courses, I think they may be required!

➢ Clean up as you go along: wash bowls, pots and utensils as soon as practical (at the very least, stack them neatly by the sink).

➢ Do not leave glasses or knives in a sink/bowl of water – someone else may find them with bloody results!

➢ Quickly rinse all saucepans and oven dishes as soon as you serve – it will make later cleaning so much easier BUT never plunge piping hot dishes into water as they may crack or shatter, especially cast-iron pots.

➢ Make friends with your dishwasher, it will be your new best friend: always keep the filters clean, and top up with salt and rinse aid regularly (otherwise glasses especially will come out looking cloudy).

➢ Always rinse off excess food from plates/cutlery etc before loading into the dishwasher, you can then often get away with a quick-cycle wash.

➢ Consider doing a quick-cycle wash after clearing the main course dishes, leaving glasses and dessert crockery for a second wash before you finish for the evening.

➢ Always check you've set the dishwasher going before you leave the chalet – it's so easy to forget.

➢ Do not overload the dishwasher, ensure each item will get fully sprayed.

➢ Do not put sharp knives in the dishwasher as it blunts their edges and is potentially dangerous when unloading.

➢ If the cutlery basket is of the type that cutlery stands on end then mix up the cutlery in each basket compartment so that spoons don't stick together and evade washing on both sides.

➢ Ensure the rotating sprayers are free to spin before starting the dishwasher.

➢ Unload the bottom rack of a dishwasher before the top rack, otherwise surplus water from the top will drip over dry dishes below.

➢ It's unlikely you'll have space for pots & pans & large utensils in the dishwasher so wash these by hand as soon as practical after use.

- When washing up in the sink: scrape off the worst of the muck and rinse all the pots/pans etc before you start washing up (your washing water will then stay cleaner); wash the cleanest things first, leaving the mucky stuff till last; change the water frequently otherwise you'll just distribute the fat and grime over every dish.
- Kettles rarely need descaling as the mountain water is quite soft but proprietary tablets do the job when needed.

Changeover Day

On changeover days you will need to clean the chalet thoroughly before the arrival of new guests. In addition to the normal cleaning don't forget to:
- check drawers and cupboards for things the guests have left behind (look underneath and on top too)
- pull out all furniture and look for rubbish, e.g. tissues down the side of beds
- vacuum/wash the floors
- clean windows
- remove all old papers & rubbish
- use anti-bacterial spray on all touch-points, e.g. light switches and door handles
- clean loos thoroughly and wash underneath and behind them too
- clean baths, showers and tiled areas
- bleach loo brushes
- clean air vents
- remove plugs and traps in sinks, removing all hair
- change bed linen & towels
- change/replenish bathroom supplies, e.g. loo-paper, soap
- check all light bulbs
- disinfect bins & install new bin-liners

Save time by making beds like a professional chambermaid: start with the duvet cover inside out; slip your hands inside and up into the top corners; with your *covered hands,* grab the duvet by its corners and hold your arms up high; give it all a bit of a shake and the cover will fall down over the duvet.

You need to find a changeover system that works for you, and it might depend on the size of the chalet or dependencies on other people. Maybe you tackle rooms 1-by-1 or maybe you do the same task in all rooms before moving to the next task.
This is how we tackle it:
- one of us cleans the kitchen, living spaces, common areas (boot rooms etc), whilst the other concentrates on the bedrooms
- firstly, cover hands liberally with pre-work barrier cream (and re-apply if you have a break and wash your hands)
- for bedrooms:
    - strip all old bed linen & towels and despatch to the laundry
    - pull-out all furniture & remove all rubbish and stuff left behind
    - check for tips left on chests/shelves!
    - keep left-over shampoos and anything else useful
    - hoover/sweep all rooms
    - don rubber gloves
    - clean all touch-points
    - clean/polish all furniture
    - clean each bathroom
    - mop all floors
    - remove rubber gloves
    - make all beds

- dress all rooms with towels, soaps etc
> for kitchen & other areas:
  - clean cupboards inside & outside
  - scrub tables, clean chairs
  - clean sofas
  - clean shelves & ornaments & pictures
  - clean touch-points
  - empty bins
  - clean TVs, videoplayers etc
  - clean fireplaces
  - vacuum &/or mop floors
> lastly, cover hands liberally with post-work moisturiser cream

And don't forget to clean **yourself** up before the new guests arrive!

Laundry

You may have a washing machine in the chalet for your personal clothes or you may have use of one in another chalet or residential unit. You may be expected to wash tea-towels and maybe hand-towels.

Guests' own laundry is usually their problem, not yours; if you offer to do it then you risk complaints if you damage it. We've always had a washing-machine in our chalets but we tell our guests (if they ask) that we use a lot of bleach for tea-towels etc and so are not able to wash guests' clothes.

Sheets, duvet covers and pillow-cases are normally sent to a local laundry.
Easy-peasy?
No, it's always a nightmare – every single year!
Sheets come back with large dirty boot prints on them, or they get bobbly and trap hairs (nice!!); pillowcases are returned with blood stains; you get someone else's laundry mixed up with yours; even *clean* items may have small black spots, and rarely do you get the right number of items returned.
Who knows why?
There's not a great deal you can do but consider:
> keep a few spares of everything (of course, if everyone does this then there may be a scarcity of supply, but only the switched-on hosts do this)
> where possible, turn items top-to-bottom, or upside down to hide any small marks
> keep spare pillows in wardrobes rather than putting 2 pillows on each bed (often only 1 is used but you have to change both if they've been in contact with guests)
> if possible, check the laundry as soon as it's delivered rather than on changeover day (in practise, this is very difficult without ending up with a screwed-up heap!)

Recycling

French resorts all operate some level of rubbish recycling so it's necessary to separate cardboard, tins, bottles etc and deposit them in the *poubelles* (usually small shelters with rubbish facilities). In Austria, recycling is serious – you are charged for all non-recyclable rubbish so sorting is very important!

So that's cooking and cleaning taken care of. The rest must be plain sailing surely?
Well, it would be if it wasn't for those people called *Guests*.

Your guests will either make or break your season – it's up to you. If you treat them as a necessary nuisance then they won't add much to your experience. But if you treat them as potential friends (or at least, not hostiles) then they can add massively to your enjoyment. And after all, it is part of your job to ensure your guests enjoy their stay with you – they've paid a great deal of money AND are paying your wages.

Welcome

Your welcome should start the minute your guests appear, which could be a knock on your chalet door as your company rep or driver delivers your new guests, or it could be when the coach enters your resort. The very second the guests see you, they will begin to form their opinions and first opinions are very difficult to alter – so make them good.

In fact, your welcome should start before the guests arrive. Even though you're knackered from changeover cleaning, ensure you are clean and smart, paint on a smile and adopt a cheery manner. Be as helpful and cheerful as possible when guests arrive. This doesn't mean carrying all their luggage (unless your company insists you do) but you could carry the odd ski-bag.

Whatever you tell them, make it upbeat, but don't lie. If the weather forecast is lousy for the week then emphasise that mountain weather changes by the minute. If the pistes are worn out then tell them you had a great day yesterday. Don't prattle but don't let an embarrassing silence descend over the chalet. Don't ask open questions that may have negative responses, e.g. *did you have a nice trip?* It's better to make positive statements or questions whose response doesn't matter either way, e.g. *have you skied here before?*

You will be busy showing people to their rooms and answering questions about meal times, ski hire, ski lessons, shopping, restaurants etc and much of what they need to know is covered by the *Welcome Speech*.

Welcome speech

Most companies will expect you to give a 'welcome speech' on the first night. This is your chance to officially welcome the guests, give them information and establish an open relationship. It can be difficult to find the best time: sometimes it works as soon as they've settled into their rooms; before dinner when you serve canapés usually works, or between dessert and coffee while they are still sitting at the table. Try to make it a 2-way exchange rather than a schoolmasterly lecture – I sit with them rather than standing aloof - and remember that humour usually works but it's not universal!

It will probably seem a bit daunting at first, but it gets easier with practice. Keep your chat informal, informative and as short as you can; it's a good idea to have a few key points written down to prompt you, at least until you get used to it, e.g.:
- welcome to our chalet, we're here to help you enjoy your holiday
- chalet rules (no smoking, no outdoor shoes….)
- fire exits
- meal times
- day off (suggest that they book a restaurant)
- keys, door codes, phone numbers
- local information (buses, lift opening times, ski schools and hire shops…)
- any special dietary requirements/likes/dislikes?
- any questions?

You might also like to request that guests stay out of the kitchen while you are cooking, and ask them not to pinch food from the fridge but guests may react badly to being treated like prisoners in a *gulag!* Some companies have a printed sheet in the guest rooms showing the basic rules, which makes your speech much shorter and less authoritarian. Really, you have to gauge the *temperature* and cover what's essential before they get bored and start talking over you.

We always end our speech with an open invitation to tell us of any problems, at any time. This helps to stop problems escalating and negates guests' complaints raised after they get home. Our closing line is often: *"we want you to have a great week because then we will too."*

Don't be surprised if they have forgotten it all by the following morning, and ask you the same questions all over again. They will expect you to know all about the resort, the pistes, the best restaurants…but if you don't know, don't bullshit. Tell them where they can find out (tourist office, rep coming in later etc) and find out yourself so that you'll know next time.

Hosting

The size of the chalet has a direct bearing on the social dynamics. You will probably be hosting alone for up to ten guests, as a couple for up to eighteen guests, or as a team for anything bigger. Small chalets may be booked by a single party – maybe a bunch of mates or an extended family. Most chalets are sometimes let to several small parties who will not know each other. Part of your role is to ensure that no one guest spoils another guest's holiday.

A chalet host doesn't need to entertain the guests with jokes and conjuring tricks - but if you can then why not? Any joke can be turned into a chalet joke by prefixing it with *"We had a guest once..."*
   "...who stopped at every airport and passport control office for a swig of whisky – he was a borderline alcoholic!"
   "...who ate a whole packet of curry powder – she's still in intensive care, in a korma!"
   "...who ate all our potatoes, the ones with eyes in – they were supposed to see us thru the week!"
And of course, there are the classic snowman jokes:
   What did one snowman say to the other? Can you smell carrots?
   What do snowmen eat? Iceburgers.
   What do snowmen wear on their heads? Icecaps.

A good host *oils the works* and ensures a pleasant atmosphere in the chalet and this can vary according to the profile of the guests. You will get some straight-laced types who *are not amused* and you'll get some who'll be a *laugh a minute.* Just be yourself.

We make a point of learning guests' names on the first day and call them by their Christian names rather than *Mrs Jones* etc. However in some companies this may be frowned upon as they wish to establish a "master-servant" relationship.

In our chalet we have a few puzzles and brain-teasers in the chalet file for guests to muse over when they have time before dinner. If the mood is right we host a quiz after dinner one night themed round snow and skiing – it can get very competitive! We also have a few card tricks and other challenges up our sleeves, which we've gleaned from other hosts or found on Google. Do whatever you feel comfortable with. To be honest, we did none of these things in our first year but our repertoire has grown over the years.

Guest book

We keep a book in which guests can write their comments before they leave. We put this on show for the new arrivals as guests like to read what others have said and it puts them in a relaxed mood if it's full of positive comments (they rarely write anything negative). It makes a lovely keepsake for you, as well as an addition to your CV.

Chalet notice board

If you can make up a chalet notice board or file, it may save a lot of questions during the week. You could include:

➢ piste map
➢ town plan
➢ bus times
➢ phone numbers (for chalet, rep, resort manager, piste security)
➢ details of shops, ski schools, ski hire shops, medical centre, restaurants

Difficult guests

"All our guest give us pleasure: some by arriving – some by leaving."

Difficult guests are a rarity. Human nature makes most people want to like and be liked, and generally everyone is in a good mood because they are on holiday. But…and it is a big but……there are a few who just seem to wind you up the wrong way. These range from harmless show-offs (*all the gear and no idea*) to bullying alpha-males. Try not to get off to a bad start with any guests; first impressions are very important. People generally decide what they think of somebody within the first few seconds of meeting them; if you get off to a bad start, it may take you the rest of the week to overcome that initial impression.

Problems always seem worse in times of stress. For example, if your new guests have had a really awful journey, they may get upset at the least little thing; if they have prolonged bad weather during the week, they can obsess about a minor irritation. Sometimes there is a real problem that needs fixing; at other times the problem may be imaginary, a matter of perception or simply blown out of proportion.

You can't do a lot about the factors that affect their stress levels. Even the most dedicated chalet host has no control over the weather, so your handling of the problem is crucial.

Firstly, acknowledge the issue, even if it is not your fault. This doesn't mean that you or your company immediately accept any blame, rather it means that you understand that the guest perceives a problem. Maintain eye contact with the guest who is complaining.

Secondly, do your best to remedy it, going beyond what you think is strictly necessary. If you are empowered to fix it, e.g. poor cleaning, then fix it quickly. If you are not so empowered, e.g. broken fixtures, then ensure the problem is escalated to the relevant person, e.g. maintenance man; but don't then wash your hands of the problem; stay in the loop until the problem is resolved. Never make any promises that you are not 100% sure you can keep, and do not promise any sort of financial compensation.

Thirdly, communicate, communicate, and communicate; if this doesn't work, call your manager and let him take the flak!

Don't criticise your company, even if you have some sympathy with the guest; as far as he is concerned, you are the face of the company.

It is important to look at each issue in terms of *who is responsible for the solution?* If you have the power to resolve the problem then do so as soon as possible and prevent it becoming a formal complaint, e.g.
➢ Guest complains about dirty room: ask them to be more specific & re-clean as appropriate if you've missed the dirt in the changeover clean
➢ Guest complains about poor food: ask the other guests for their opinion – it may be just one fussy guest; if you've really cocked up then possibly offer to substitute something quick from the freezer

Sometimes the problem is not actually yours to resolve but is the guests' own problem, e.g. where a party have booked the whole chalet then if a guest complains about chalet noise in the night then it's really up to the party leader to resolve this one.

Some problems have different solutions depending on the nature of the bookings, e.g. if you have a noise complaint with multiple independent bookings in the chalet then it becomes your problem, so ask the guests to respect each other's 'right to quiet'.

If you can't agree with your guest on a satisfactory outcome to a problem then you'll have to involve your manager. Your manager should also be informed immediately if a problem arises that you have no power to resolve, e.g.

➢ Guest doesn't like their room: even if you have a spare suitable room you may not know if it will be booked by your office for a latecomer

➢ Guest feels the website is misleading: you should be familiar with the website contents for your company and your chalet; if a guest has an issue then you can try to diffuse it but ultimately it's a management problem.

Having escalated the problem through your management, remember to keep your guest informed of any progress so far.

Don't let a guest bully you, and avoid being "cornered in the kitchen" - try to have all discussions in earshot of another guest or member of staff then you've a witness to what was said, and often another guest might intervene to defuse the situation.

As a sweeping generalisation, older hosts will have less issues with troublesome guests than younger hosts. This is partly because they've more experience in handling people but also because guests are less likely *to try it on* in the first place. The nightmare scenario for younger hosts is a group of guests about your own age who just want to make you feel small – it's tough but just don't rise to the bait.

Always remember that they'll be gone soon whereas you have the rest of the season to have fun.

Remember too: *The customer is always right* even when you know he's not. Keep calm and be as pleasant as you can but don't be browbeaten by bullies - you are their host, not their slave.

A Magic Recipe for Good Guests
Take a pinch of positive thinking
And a spoonful of solicitude
Mix in a knob of nonchalance
With a bucketful of luck
Sprinkle generously with stardust
Simmer for a week
And keep your fingers crossed

MISCELLANEOUS

LEFTOVERS

At first you may be horrified by the quantities of food that you throw away. You cannot risk having too little food and it is very difficult to gauge the amounts that will be needed. With experience you will get better at judging quantities, but you will still inevitably have some food left over.

Leftovers should not be served to guests but some leftovers will be fine for you to eat and there are usually other staff such as maintenance guys, reps, drivers and ski-hire shop-workers who will appreciate handouts. These people don't always have their food included as part of their deal, and it is well worth keeping them sweet!

It is a good idea to wash and keep empty containers such as jars and tubs; they can be used to keep leftovers in – but make sure you label them (permanent marker is best).

> ➤ Consider using leftovers in canapés.
> ➤ Roast meat such as pork is great for lunchtime sandwiches.
> ➤ Bread can be used to make croutons, crostinis or breadcrumbs (best made by grating old *frozen* baguette); or used for bruschettas, and stale bread is fine for French toasts at breakfast .
> ➤ Potatoes can be fried or made into potato cakes for breakfast.
> ➤ Uneaten vegetables can be frozen and later made into soup.
> ➤ Scrap raw pastry can be rolled with cheese and baked into cheese straws.
> ➤ Pancakes can be frozen and then defrosted and flashed in a hot pan to reheat.
> ➤ Fresh fruit that is beginning to go off can be used in a fruit salad.
> ➤ .....use your imagination!

COPING WITH DISASTERS

You would be extremely lucky to get through a season without a single disaster. It's how you cope with them that matters! Try not to panic, do your utmost to keep the guests happy and accept help from any available source. Although it might seem like an unmitigated disaster at the time, it probably won't seem so bad in retrospect.

Food disasters range from recipes that just didn't turn out right, through forgetting that you have a guest allergic to onions, to dropping the casserole as you take it out of the oven!

Generally speaking, guests are not in a hurry to get on with their meals, so you can usually buy time by making sure they have plenty of wine! Be honest with them and apologise when things have gone really wrong. Don't try to lay the blame elsewhere, and don't castigate yourself too much. We are all human and we all make mistakes.

There may be other chalets close by who can help you out, or possibly you could phone a manager or rep for assistance. Guests can be very helpful too!

The best way to be prepared for food disasters is to keep some emergency rations. A microwave is invaluable for speedy cooking of small portions, and quick defrosting.

> ➤ Small frozen fish fillets can be fried quickly.
> ➤ Frozen peas or beans will be cooked in a few minutes.
> ➤ A single jacket potato only takes about 5 minutes in the microwave.
> ➤ Pasta dishes are quick and delicious. (e.g. penne alla salmone).
> ➤ Confit de canard can be stored for ages and served within half an hour.

➢ Part-baked bread can be kept for ages in the cupboard and cooked in the oven quickly when the baker can't get through the fresh snow!

For quick desserts try:
➢ Ice cream with meringues and raspberries.
➢ Eton Mess (smashed up meringues, raspberries and cream).
➢ Banana splits (see recipe section for quick chocolate sauce).
➢ Raspberries swirled with natural yoghurt or fromage frais.

Coping with small "disasters":
➢ Lumpy sauces, soups etc: try whisking/beating, or simply sieve it.
➢ Burnt porridge in base of pan (or sauces etc): taste it and if OK carefully transfer it to another pan without scraping the bottom, but if it tastes burnt or has black bits in it then throw it away and start again
➢ Burnt cake (or cake has risen lop-sided etc): provided it's not a pile of ash (!) then cut off the burnt bits and coat generously with icing, and consider turning it upside down to get a flat top. If it's irrecoverable then use one of the Country Fruit Loaves that you put in reserve earlier (didn't you?) or knock up some flapjacks in 15 minutes.
➢ Canapés spoilt: serve olives, peanuts etc or quickly make bruschettas.
➢ Fussy last-minute guests (e.g. I don't like duck): keep individually frozen chicken breasts in reserve.

FIRES

Many chalets have a log fire that you will have to manage. If you get it right then it creates a warm cosy atmosphere to relax your guests, but if you get it wrong then you risk smoking them out and literally creating a bad atmosphere. If you understand that a fire needs three things: dry fuel, plenty of air, and a light, then you shouldn't go too far wrong.

➢ store logs outside, out of the snow – surprisingly they will dry out
➢ bring enough logs indoors each day (keep 1 or 2 days supply in hand) to dry out by the fire (or in warmth of chalet)
➢ keep kindling (i.e. sticks & small offcuts) as dry as possible (wooden crates from the *poubelles* are great, or chop pieces off any logs that split easily)
➢ don't leave surplus kindling by the fire – guests will burn your entire supply in 1 night!
➢ rake out ash each morning & leave in metal container outside until cold before disposal (do not leave container on wooden balconies)
➢ lighting the fire:
  o screw up newspaper into loose balls and lay in centre of grate (4-6 sheets)
  o place torn-up cardboard in a wigwam fashion on the paper (egg boxes are great, also cereal boxes etc); don't lay cardboard sheets across the paper as they'll prevent the upward airflow
  o cover with kindling, in a wigwam fashion
  o place 2 or 3 small/thin logs to complete the wigwam
  o select more logs of smallish size but don't add them yet
  o light paper in 3 or 4 places
  o if the fire has a door then close it but ensure air-holes are fully open (it may be better to leave door ajar)
  o wait!
  o when logs have caught fire, add further logs
  o leave air-holes open for at least 15 minutes
➢ managing the fire:
  o it's tempting to throw on lots of logs as soon as a flame appears – don't!
  o waiting for the fire to catch is a pain, it's tempting to go off and cook something – don't (the fire will have burnt out by the time you remember)

- adjust the air-holes once the fire is established – how much depends on your fire, it's trial and error but don't create a blast-furnace that's uncomfortable to sit in
- remember to add logs during dinner (it's very easy to forget and all the guests have left over coffee is a pile of ash!)
- don't let guests light the fire (you can't practically stop them putting on logs); this is usually an insurance constraint
- on day-off, consider removing kindling etc if you can't trust your guests
- get a good fire going before your guests arrive on the first day, it'll earn you maximum brownie points
- depending on how warm your chalet is, you may not need it every night BUT if the guests want it then light it

Fireplaces will need cleaning too, in particular fire-glass gets sooty and stained with wood-resin. Try rubbing it hard with newspaper, then use proprietary products and soft-cloths. If you use abrasive scourers then it will leave scratches that will simply attract more dirt.

HONESTY BARS

Many chalet companies operate an honesty bar that stocks beers, colas, mixers, and maybe some nibbles. Guests help themselves and either pay-as-they-go, or keep a tab of their dues and settle-up on departure day. Companies vary as to how the bar is operated: some provide the stock and take all the income, some expect you to provide the stock from your own money and you keep all the income, some have a system half-way in between. Clearly, if you get to keep the profit then it's worth doing, and you can often make 30 euros a week profit. If you don't get the profit then it's just a pain that must be endured. Honesty Bars are popular with most guests.

- keep it well-stocked – a half-empty bar shows you don't care (and you'll lose potential profit); this applies all through the week, not just on changeover day
- keep stock cool; often there'll be a dedicated fridge, otherwise balconies can be useful (keep away from the fire)
- keep it clean at all times
- keep receipts for all stock purchases and ensure they're paid for from the right funds (chalet budget or your own – it depends)
- if you're able to, price all items the same for simplicity (1 euro is usual)
- bottles of water can be sold for use during the day (they cost over 2 euros on the slopes)
- chocolate bars are also popular
- don't allow guests to mix up their own beer & nibbles with your stock (you can try to discourage them buying their own beer but they will anyway)
- check the takings (or tab) against the stock after the first night, and again mid-week; don't be afraid to say (politely) if things don't tally
- collect any tabs on the last night preferably, as the departure morning may be frantic; ensure you have loose change in case a guest presents euro notes
- run stocks down at end of season or you'll be left with unsold stock, paid for with your money (in practice, this is very hard to do without having a half-empty bar – you may just have to drink the unsold beer in your close-down period!)

SAUNAS AND JACUZZIS

Many chalets have saunas and jacuzzis and at first you think – wow! Unfortunately, you are often forbidden from using them due to potential health risks, and the ethos of some companies that guests don't mix with staff (at least, not that intimately!). You will be trained in their operation during your set-up period.

A few things to note about saunas:
- they must be scrubbed/hosed/disinfected on changeover day even though they don't look dirty; lift and clean drain covers & any other mats etc

- every day ensure the water-bucket is full
- if there is a timing device, it's a nice touch to have it turned on ready for the returning skiers (program it to turn off at night if possible)

A few things to note about jacuzzis:
- the acidity & chlorine levels must be carefully managed to maintain a healthy environment; this normally involves testing and adjusting the water three times a day
- some companies empty/clean/refill them on each changeover day, whilst some do this every month, or even once a season
- do not allow guests to take glasses or bottles into the water (you won't see the broken glass until it's too late); provide plastic beakers etc – if they're not too tacky then people will use them, if you provide paper cups then likely they'll be ignored
- remember to close the lid at the end of each session to conserve the heat (guests are hopeless at this)
- keep a safe path clear of snow/ice to outdoor jacuzzis (quite difficult in practice)

And also note:
- consider how you'll manage the wet guests dripping through the chalet to their bedrooms
- even if you restrict sauna/jacuzzi sessions to set times, the guests will still use them in the middle of the night, when they're drunk, with their new-found girlfriend etc etc - so just live with it – it's their holiday after all
- do not be afraid to (politely) advise guests about any unsuitable behaviour that could affect other guests

AND FINALLY... MAKING THE MOST OF IT

In order to get the most out of being a chalet host, you need to be sociable, enthusiastic and enjoy cooking. The key skill you will need for a successful season is ORGANISATION. After all, the main reason for being there is the snow; so you want to spend the minimum amount of time running your chalet, and maximise your powder time. On the other hand, you are being paid to do a job, and if you don't do it well, you will be letting down your guests, your employer and yourself – and you may find yourself shipped back home at your own expense.

If you are flying out, your luggage allowance will be meagre, so you will need to be as economical as possible with your belongings! Even if you travel out by coach, space will be limited and there is always a possibility that you will return by air. However, shopping in ski resorts tends to be limited and expensive, and you don't want to have to spend your hard earned cash unnecessarily. If you are taking your own skis or board, book ahead with the airline (costs much less than excess luggage at the airport).

If you drive to resort then you can take what you like but it's an expensive option and can be problematic. Companies may pay a small contribution but you'll have to cover fuel and toll costs, as well as breakdown insurance and maybe overnight accommodation en route. Consider where you'll park – a car that's left in the snow unused for five months is probably not going to be happy! You may also become a convenient taxi for all your mates.

It's similar to going on a long holiday, so you will probably want to take things like a camera, books, music player and computer (and a supply of DVDs might be handy for whiteout or worn-out days). An alarm clock or watch is essential, and a calculator for doing your budget paperwork. Nowadays, a smart-phone does the lot.

You do not need loads of clothes; most of your time will be spent either in uniform or ski gear, but make sure you have enough basics to see you through till washing time! Most companies provide washing machines for staff use. If possible, take easy-care clothes that can be tumble dried; you will be doing plenty of housework without adding hand washing or ironing!

Obviously you will need ski gear: jacket, salopettes, gloves, socks, helmet or hat, scarf or snood, thermals, fleeces; a backpack is really handy. Ski wear (along with almost everything else) is usually very expensive in resort, so it's cheaper to buy in the UK before you go. Most ski shops have heavily discounted end of season sales, so if possible, buy in late spring! TK Maxx often has some good bargains during the winter, also checkout Lidls, if you are not bothered about having this year's model.

Most chalets are kept fairly warm and you will probably be surprised at how few really warm clothes you need, apart from ski gear. Most people exist in jeans, tshirts and hoodies/sweatshirts with the occasional dressy outfit for going out. You will probably be expected to have a fairly smart pair of black trousers for your uniform; make sure that they are comfortable, not too warm and easily washable. It is a good idea to have some lightweight clothes for chalet cleaning, which you'll probably bin at the end of season.

I would not be without a warm, waterproof pair of boots and a really comfy pair of shoes for working in. You may want to take some rubber crampons that slip over boots (about £10 from Amazon).

Towards the end of the season it will get quite warm; take shorts, a hat and flip-flops for soaking up those rays. It is probably worth taking a swimming costume too, in case you want to use a pool or spa.

The equipment in most chalet kitchens is fairly basic, so you may wish to take things such as knives or an electric whisk/blender, and a kitchen timer is always useful.

I always take a waterproof magic-marker, blu-tack, post-it notes and a plentiful supply of pens (I don't know where they go to ...perhaps they get taken by the goblins!). And photos of family and friends are absolutely essential to me.

Take as much moisturiser (especially for hands) as you can; the altitude combined with the work will play havoc with your skin. You will need plenty of sunscreen, mostly for your face, and lip-balm. Obviously you should take any special medicines that you might need. Pharmacies tend to be expensive so if you are fussy about cosmetics (shampoo etc), take as much as you can; basic painkillers such as ibuprofen are relatively expensive too, so take a few for those aching muscles and bruises!

If you are at all handy, it may be worth taking a very basic tool kit (screwdriver, sharp knife and pliers or mole grips) as it will save you having to call out maintenance for easy repair jobs. Don't forget to take adaptor plugs and chargers for electrical items.

In terms of paperwork, you will need your passport and EHIC for EU countries. Also take your contract of employment and your driving licence if there is any chance that you might need to drive. Most UK bank cards can be used at cash machines throughout Europe. You will probably need some passport sized photos for your ski pass too.

If you have arranged your own insurance, take the details with you. Insurance is absolutely vital. You will need cover for your belongings, travel, accident and health. If your company provides insurance as part of the deal, check that it covers everything. You should seriously consider taking out special ski insurance to get you off the mountain if you have an accident. In Europe this is known as Carte Neige, available from lift pass offices. Some resorts have their own (often cheaper) schemes as well. Although standard winter sports insurance should eventually cover the cost of being brought down on the blood wagon (or even helicopter), you will have to pay the charges at the time and claim it back from your insurance company – and that's a lot of hassle at a time of maximum stress.

Before you go, get set up for internet banking if possible and ensure any household bills get paid while you're away. And maybe get someone to monitor your post.

Lifestyle benefits of being a chalet host

First, the pros:
➢ Skiing (up to 6 days a week; ski pass and equipment provided)
➢ Food and lodging provided
➢ No bills (fuel, transport, council tax etc)
➢ No commuting to work
➢ Free or reduced price ski tuition
➢ Clean healthy environment
➢ Chance to improve your cooking and organisational skills
➢ Opportunity to make new friends for life
➢ Interesting guests, some of whom may be business people who might have openings in their companies for someone just like you

And now the cons:
➢ Long way from home and family
➢ May be addictive (but at least it is better for your health and wealth than gambling, drinking or drugs)
➢ Poor pay
➢ Bad guests!
➢ Cleaning loos
➢ Lack of personal space
➢ Risk of injury (so get insured, don't take stupid risks and keep your fingers crossed)

For us, the pros far outweigh the cons, but it pays to be aware of the disadvantages before you commit yourself to 5 months in a foreign country.

You certainly won't get rich being a chalet host, but you do get virtually all your living expenses covered. Depending on how much après ski you partake in, you could live on your tips and save the actual salary.

You will be able to ski (or board!) for several hours on most days; your equipment and lift pass will be provided as part of the package, and you will probably be able to arrange free or reduced price lessons. You don't need to be a good skier; in fact if you have never hit the slopes this is a great opportunity to learn a new skill.

Most of the guests are lovely, friendly people and some will become good friends. They are all there because they love skiing, so you will always have something in common. Inevitably there will be some who you simply do not like; all you can do is to maintain a professional attitude and look forward to changeover day! They are unlikely to be with you for more than a week. In extreme cases, we adopt a survival mantra: *take delivery at start of week, process them during the week, despatch at end of week*

We've only ever met one person who enjoys cleaning loos (don't go there!)…. so just grin and bear it. Take pride in the fact that you are doing a good job.

The lack of personal space bothers some people more than others. Most seasonnaires have to share accommodation, and some of it is fairly basic. If you apply as a couple (either romantically or just friends) you will probably get a room together; otherwise you may well have to share with a complete stranger (or two), which often works really well and leads to lifelong friendships. If you decide to apply with a partner or friend, bear in mind that you could be together 24/7; this can put quite a strain on relationships. Be honest with yourselves; can you stand to work, sleep and play together?

Some chalets have live-in accommodation for staff, which saves time walking to and from work, and leads to a more inclusive feel with guests. On the other hand, the guests will know that you are there all the time, so you are never really off duty (and nobody likes being woken at 8am on their day off to be asked how the coffee maker works!)

Some chalet hosts live in separate staff accommodation. This means that you live with other like minded people, and it can be more fun, especially for young chalet hosts. On the downside, it can be messy and noisy and you will probably have to walk a short distance to work. We've known staff living literally on a shelf in an office behind a curtain so you can't be picky.

During the season, you will probably learn more about yourself than you anticipate. You will have a considerable amount of responsibility; and very often the buck stops with you! As far as the guests are concerned, you are the face of the company; it is up to you to make sure that they get good value and enjoyment from the considerable sum of money that they have spent on their ski holiday. You need to appear cheerful and confident all the time, and be flexible when things go wrong. Running a chalet single-handed shouldn't be undertaken lightly – occasionally you will feel alone and desperate. But there will always be staff and friends to support you; so you need never feel lonely or alone.

Some ski companies like their hosts to eat with the guests. This can be enjoyable, but it does make dinner much longer and takes a lot more planning. A good compromise is to only eat the main course, or sit down with the guests for coffee, when you can relax a bit. To be honest, if you ate the full 3 course meal every night for an entire season, you would go home several sizes larger. The term "*chalet host's bum*" wasn't coined for nothing!

Some hosts prefer to eat their dinner later, once they have finished work. Each to his own, but it doesn't work for me. If I haven't eaten before I cook the guests' dinner, I pick at leftovers, eat all the wrong types of food and then don't fancy a proper meal. It is important to look after yourself and eat well; without having too much rich food. You are leading a very active lifestyle, so you will probably need more food than you do normally….but nobody wants to go home several sizes larger.

Often you will have left over food from the previous night (you cannot serve leftovers to the guests, but if you store them carefully they will be fine for you!) Other times you will find yourself craving plain and simple food.

One of the best things about having children to stay is that you can eat comfort food like them (pasta, fish pie, pizza ….)

The downside of having child guests is that it's more work for you. You normally prepare a separate meal for them at an earlier time and in general they make a lot more mess. And if they have nannies then your chalet becomes a playground – possibly for all the kids on the block! Sometimes you can persuade the parents that everyone could eat together at an earlier time but where the guests are a mix of groups all parties might not agree. Often parents want to *get rid of the kids* for the evening. In practise, the kids often hang around all evening regardless of when they eat. Remember, it's not your job to literally feed the children – that's the parents' job - put their food on the table and make yourself scarce or parents may say "*can you just feed little Johnny for me*" (while they languish in the hot tub!)

Try to be flexible if your guests want different meal times; for example if they want to go to a firework display one night. However, it's best to get all guests in a mixed booking to eat at the same time otherwise your work will double. Keep in mind that you are running a chalet with fixed meal times and menu, not a hotel, so don't let your guests dictate to you!

Guests often like to linger around the table after they have finished eating. Unfortunately this prevents you from clearing the table properly, which can mean an unwelcome mess first thing in the morning. If you can, encourage the guests to clear their glasses to the sink before they go to bed, and put any remaining wine, cheese, butter, milk etc in the fridge. If you have a suitable coffee table in the sitting area then you can try moving your guests away from the dining table but in practise we've found you sometimes need a bulldozer!

Try to make good use of any slack time while you are on duty. There is usually something you can do to ease the next day's workload instead of standing around waiting. Keep a piece of paper stuck inside one of your cupboard doors; write down anything you need to buy next time you shop. We also keep a copy of the menu plan there for quick reference.

Changeover day is completely different; you might be up at 4am to see guests off, and not finish until midnight. In addition to the usual chores, you have to thoroughly clean the entire chalet, change the beds and still be bright and cheerful to greet your new guests. Open the doors and windows, turn up the music and keep looking out to remind yourself what a fabulous view you have from the office! Try to get a rest during the day or you will be shattered long before you can get to bed.

All chalet staff have one day off each week (lucky ones may get an additional morning). On your day off the guests usually help themselves to a cold breakfast and afternoon tea which you lay out the night before; in more expensive chalets there may be relief hosts to do your work. Guests usually go out for dinner at a local restaurant; in busy weeks they will need to book a table in advance, so remind them a day or two beforehand. Ensure that there is plenty of cereal, juice, jam, milk, butter etc (and remember to leave extra loo rolls in the bathrooms). If relevant, tell them where the bread is delivered.

Show them how to use the dishwasher (you don't want to come in to a pile of dirty dishes on the following morning) and make sure they have an emergency contact number (usually the resort manager).

If you're running the chalet by yourself then it's hard work as you have to do everything – but at least you can do it your way. If you are working with another person(s) then it's important to identify the roles each of you must play. Your company may dictate that one of you cooks and the other cleans and hosts as well as possibly helping with meal preparation. This should work fine in practise providing everyone pulls their weight! Use the Timing Plan (see separate section) to allocate who cooks what for clarity. One person should be in overall charge of the whole meal to ensure everything is done and nothing is missed (it's too easy to assume that *someone* has done the spuds and miss them out altogether!). That head person assigns tasks to others and checks they've been done, as well as doing their own tasks; they coordinate everything to meet the timing plan. Of course, it can be a different person for each meal. If you don't assign a *head cook* for your meal then remember the adage "too many cooks spoil the broth"!

There are three basic elements to chalet hosting: working, skiing and socialising. Most of the book covers the work aspect, but we've saved the best till last! The last two are what you are really in the mountains for!

Once you have the work aspect organised, you can really enjoy yourself on and off the slopes. You have a whole season to enjoy the snow. You should be able to get out on the slopes 5 or 6 days a week. You will generally not be able to ski on changeover day, and your time may be limited on shopping day. On working days, try to get back in time for a shower/rest/cuppa before you are on duty again.

A word of warning: if for '*socialising*' you read '*drinking*', please exercise a bit of caution. It's possible to excel at any two of the three elements (work, ski, socialise), but not all three at the same time. The work aspect is non-negotiable; if you don't do a reasonable job you will be dismissed, so you need to find a balance between time spent in bars and on pistes. At the risk of sounding a real old fogey, après ski is fantastic as long as you don't get so hung-over that you have to spend all your free time in bed recovering. What a waste!

Your days off give you the chance to catch the first lift and conquer virgin powder and freshly groomed (corduroy) pistes. Quite simply, there's nothing like it! You can have the slopes virtually to yourselves until the masses get up.

If you decide to venture off piste, get the necessary information, equipment and training before setting off. Don't be talked into it on the spur of the moment by a mate. Besides being beautiful and awesome, mountains can be dangerous. In true Boy Scout tradition, '*Be prepared*'. Attend an avalanche talk if you get the opportunity, they are usually free at the start of season.

Remember that weather conditions can change quickly in the mountains. Pay heed to weather forecasts and don't go too far away if the weather is unsettled. Lifts that link adjacent valleys often close at short notice if the wind gets strong. Make sure you don't miss the last lift to get back home when your guests are depending on you for dinner!

Many ski schools offer free or cheap tuition to seasonnaires. Everyone, including experienced skiers, can benefit from lessons!

You will almost certainly find the first few weeks exhausting, exciting, disorienting – *crazy!* You may find there's no time for skiing, guests are demanding, managers are unreasonable, etc etc. There are many stressed people at the start of season as inexperienced staff are trying to get to grips with their roles. Xmas and New Year are definitely the worst as guests have paid top dollar yet are served by inexperienced staff; menus may need changing to cope with Xmas dinner, and sometimes changeover days differ depending when Xmas falls.

Stick with it!

In early January everything suddenly seems to be working properly, people relax, you know what you're doing – and there's plenty of time to ski.

Like all jobs, a big factor in how well it goes depends on your fellow team members and your management. Learn to love your team (or at least tolerate them, as they tolerate you) and don't let petty things become huge bugbears. Unlike most other jobs you are with your team almost 24x7 so tensions are almost inevitable. Your manager may be super-supportive or a total pain-in-the-ass brown-noser but *resistance is (generally) useless!* Unless your life is totally unbearable then a good whinge with your mates (out of earshot of guests and other staff) is generally a good antidote and then go skiing!!!!

Mature hosts may well find the initial experience very frustrating as they may have been used to managing far more demanding roles in their work but we strongly advise you to *button your lip* and go with the flow. We know from experience that ski companies do not want you telling them how to run their operations better; they are too busy paddling furiously to stay afloat. Save your observations for later when things have quietened down and maybe share a beer and your opinions in an informal way – but don't expect anything much to change quickly!

Around February half-term time you may feel drained and fed-up. Nearly everyone does – it's the *mid-season blues*. You've had enough. People start talking about what they'll do when they go home. They ski less. They drink more. It's very easy to be dragged down by the general apathy but you should fight it. Yes you do get tired – so give the bar a miss for a few nights. Go and do that challenging piste you've been promising yourself. Get motivated – there's still at least six-to-eight weeks left. And don't forget, your guests have paid good money and deserve good hosting in the first week, the mid weeks, and right up to the very last week.

And suddenly, it's all over – the last guests have gone. There's nothing to do but play!

Dream on!

The big closedown involves lots of cleaning and probably little skiing. You'll need to be energetic and flexible, doing extra jobs that your manager deems necessary – just when you're winding down.

It can all get a bit fractious especially if you have skivers in your team who don't pull their weight!

One big tip: before you go – get yourself fit!
You'll be on your feet a lot of the time, either in the kitchen or on skis or in a bar, and that takes a toll on your body; together with less oxygen at higher altitude, you can very soon become exhausted without actually realising it. That's when an accident is likely to happen, which could be the end of your season. So do some basic muscle toning exercises and some cardio-vascular exercises before you go – there's lots of advice on the internet.
It'll be worth it – trust us.

We hope that this book will help you to enjoy your ski season(s) as much as we do.

Remember:

ONE SEASON MIGHT NOT BE ENOUGH!

CHECK LISTS

THINGS TO TAKE WITH YOU

Clothes	Miscellaneous
underwear	Camera
socks	Mobile phone
smart trousers	Computer
cleaning clothes	Mp3 player
going out clothes	Walkie talkies (useful where mobile signal is weak)
t shirts	Batteries/chargers for all the above
sweatshirts/jumpers	DVDs/videos
jeans	Calculator
work shoes	Alarm clock
rubber crampons	Photos of family / friends
waterproof boots	Books
gloves	Guest book
shorts	Permanent marker
flip flops	Blu-tack
swimming costume	Post-it notes
	Pens
Skiwear	Dictionary or phrase book
jacket	Mains adaptor plugs
salopettes	Tools (screwdriver, sharp knife, duck tape etc)
thermals (merino wool are best)	
socks	
fleeces	**Paperwork**
back pack	Passport
hand-warmer packs	EHIC
hat/helmet	Driving licence (both parts)
gloves	Travel insurance details (try AtlasDirect.co.uk)
	Bank cards (credit and/or debit)
	Passport photos
Personal	Currency
moisturiser	Contract of employment
hand cream	
barrier cream	
shampoo	**Kitchen equipment** (ask if they are provided)
ibuprofen	knives
sunscreen	lemon zester
wash gear	apple corer
	blender / whisk
	electronic scales
	timer

DRIVING TO RESORT

o   Ensure your insurance covers driving abroad for the whole season (they're often limited to 90 days – try Saga)

o   Ensure your road tax is valid for the whole season – your insurance may be void if the tax lapses; nowadays you can tax online

o   Ensure your MoT is valid for the whole season

o   Ensure your car is serviced before you leave, especially items like antifreeze

o   Consider breakdown insurance (most have a 90 day duration per trip; checkout Britannia Rescue)

o   Consider fitting snow tyres but always take snow chains (& know how to use them), thin tough gloves (to handle the chains), kneeling mat, shovel, torch, de-icer

o   Don't let snow pile up on the car for weeks on end – the roof could buckle!

o   Drive the car every few weeks for at least 30 minutes.

o   Always park the car in 1st gear; with the handbrake disengaged or lightly engaged to prevent it freezing on; with the wipers off the screen (to prevent freezing and subsequent overload of the wiper motor); with the wheels pointing forward in case you need to fit snow chains; with the car reversed into its parking slot to allow an easier getaway in the snow.

o   Learn how to drive in the snow: watch YouTube or ask someone who knows; drive slowly in the highest gear possible and do everything smoothly, especially braking and steering.

LEAVING YOUR HOUSE EMPTY

o   Consider getting a trusted lodger

o   Get a trusted person to check the house regularly (weekly) & move mail etc from view

o   Consider re-directing mail if anything might need attention (you'll still get circulars & flyers)

o   Get online as much as possible for banking, insurances etc

o   Ensure your insurance covers an empty house for the whole period (they're often limited to 90 days – try Saga)

o   Keep a diary of anything you need to do abroad, e.g. renew house/car insurance.

o   Take a copy of important documents (passports, driving licences, insurance policies, car registration etc); either printed or on laptop/tablet or in the cloud (suitably secured)

o   Reschedule any maintenance/servicing that normally occurs during the winter, e.g. boiler checks.

o   Consider cancelling/suspending phone/broadband

o   Consider cancelling/suspending club memberships etc

o   Drain central heating or put on frost-protect program

o   Turn off water at main stopcock if possible (most boilers are OK with this), or isolate taps/pipes as far as possible, then drain as much as possible

o   Turn off outside taps & drain hosepipes

o   Empty loo cisterns if possible

o   Bleach all sinks & drains and pour in bleach again immediately before leaving

o   Ensure tanks in the loft are well lagged or drain if possible

o   Consider using a de-humidifier on a timer

o   Consider using a heater on a timer (oil-filled radiators are safest)

o   Open one or two windows just a crack for ventilation (but make them burglar-proof)

o   Oil/grease garage stuff, e.g. bikes, tools

o   Consider securing tools etc in lockable storage

o   Secure the garden against storms etc, (take in collapsible washing lines)

o   Remove batteries from clocks etc

o   Remove batteries from battery-powered smoke alarms (unless someone will respond to an alarm) or replace with new batteries to last the season

FRENCH TRANSLATIONS

Fruits & Nuts

Apple	*Pomme*
Almond	*Amande*
Apricot	*Abricot*
Banana	*Banane*
Blueberry	*Myrtille*
Cranberry	*Airelle*
Cherry	*Cerise*
Coconut	*Noix de coco*
Date	*Date*
Grapes	*Raisins*
Grapefruit	*Pamplemouse*
Hazelnuts	*Noisette*
Lemon	*Citron*
Melon	*Melon*
Orange	*Orange*
Peach	*Peche*
Pear	*Poire*
Pineapple	*Ananas*
Raspberry	*Framboise*
Strawberry	*Fraise*
Walnuts	*Noix des cerneaux*

Vegetables

Artichoke	*Artichaud*
Aubergine	*Aubertine*
Broccoli	*Calabrese*
Beans (runner)	*Haricot vert*
Cabbage	*Choux*
Carrots	*Carottes*
Cauliflower	*Chouxfleur*
Celeriac	*Celen-rave*
Chicory	*Endive*
Courgettes	*Courgettes*
Cucumber	*Concumbre*
Garlic	*Ail*
Leeks	*Poireaux*
Lettuce	*Laitue*
Mushrooms	*Champignon*
Peas	*Petits pois*
Peppers	*Poivrons*
Onions	*Oignons*
Spinach	*Epinards*
Sweetcorn	*Mais doux*
Tomatoes	*Tomates*

Dry Goods / Baking

Apple Juice	*Jus de pomme*
Raising agent	*Chemique levre*
Chick Peas	*Pois chiches*
Coffee	*Café*
Cocoa powder	*Cacao*
Sweetcorn	*Mais doux*
Cornflour	*Maizena / farine de mais*
Flour – Plain	*Farine*
Flour – raising	*Farine gateau*
Herb – Black Pepper	*Poivre noir*
Herb - Cinnamon	*Cannelle*
Herb - Ginger	*Gingembre*
Herbs – mixed	*Herbs de Provence*
Herb – Turmeric	*Curcuma*
Honey	*Miel*
Jam – Apricot	*Confiture d'abricot*
Jam – Strawberry	*Confiture de fraises*
Jelly - redcurrant	*Gelle de groseilles*
Mustard	*Moutarde*
Oil, sunflower	*Huile de tournesol*
Oil, olive	*Huile d'olive*
Orange juice	*Jus d'orange*
Porridge oats	*Gruau d'avoine*
Rice	*Riz*
Salt	*Sel*
Soya	*Soja*
Sugar – Caster	*Sucre poudre*
Sugar – Granulated	*Sucre cristal*
Sugar – Icing	*Sucre glace*
Sugar - demerara	*Cassonade*
Sugar – soft brown	*vergeoise brune*
Tea	*the*
Tinned Tomatoes, chopped	*Tomates pulpes*
Tuna	*Thon*
Vinegar	*Vinaigre*

Herbs

Chives	*Ciboulette*
Parsley	*Persil*
Rosemary	*Romarin*
Sage	*Sauge*
Thyme	*Thym*
Coriander	*Coriander*
Mint	*Menthe*

Meat & Poultry		Fish	
Bacon	*Poitrine fume*	Cod	*Cabillard*
Beef	*Boeuf*	Prawns	*Crevettes*
Chicken pieces	*Cuisses de poulet*	Salmon	*Saumon*
Chicken breasts	*Blancs de poulet*	Snails	*Escargots*
Duck	*Canard*	Sole	*Limande*
Frogs' legs	*Pattes de grenouilles*	Tuna	*Thon*
Ham	*Jambon*		
Lamb	*Agneau*		
Pork	*Porc*		
Turkey	*Dinde*		

Dairy/chilled food		Common Allergens	
Butter	*Beurre*	Nuts	*Noix*
Cheese	*Fromage*	Peanuts	*Cacahouètes*
Double cream	*Crème entiere*	Walnuts	*Noix des cerneaux*
Eggs	*Oeufs*	Milk	*Lait*
Milk (semi skimmed)	*Lait (demi ecreme)*	Dairy	*laiterie*
Milk (full fat)	*Lait (entiere)*	Eggs	*Oeufs*
Pastry (shortcrust)	*Pâte brisée*	Flour	*Farine*
Pastry (sweetened shortcrust)	*Pâte sablé*	Gluten	*Gluten*
Pastry (puff)	*Pâte feuilletée*	Soya	*Soya / soja*
		Sulphur dioxide	*Dioxyde de soufre*
		Sesame	*Sesame*
		Poppy seeds	*Graines de pavot*
		Fish	*Peche*

You have reached the end of *The Chalet Host's Bible*

Congrats, now go skiing

Get Cooking
Get Skiing
Get a Life

ALSO BY THE AUTHORS

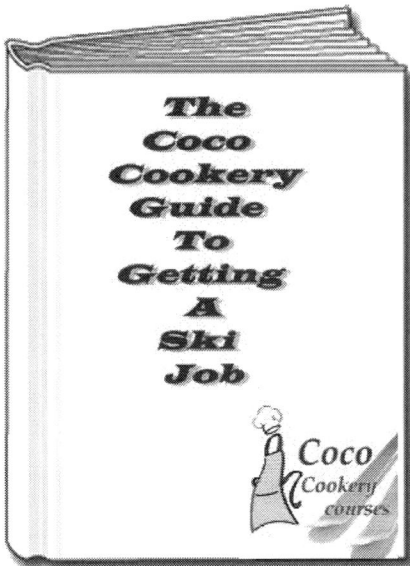

The Coco Cookery Guide To Getting A Ski Job

If you're looking to work in a ski resort this winter then this is the book for you. It tells you:

➢ how to construct a compelling CV
➢ which companies might be suitable for you
➢ how to apply for the right job
➢ what they might ask you at an interview
➢ what you should ask them at an interview

In fact it tells you everything you need to guide you through the employment maze and onto the white stuff.

Whether you want to be a chalet host, cook, nanny, maintenance man or resort manager then this is the essential book for you.

Published by Mallaktech on behalf of Coco Cookery,
www.cococookery.co.uk/jobservice.html

ABOUT THE AUTHORS

We are a married couple, Jeff and Anne, with over 10 years experience of chalet hosting in the French Alps. Before becoming addicted to life in the mountains, Jeff was an IT consultant and trainer, while Anne was a further education teacher.

We founded our Coco business in 2003 when we realised life was way too short, and so quit the rat race. We dabbled in a few things before deciding to take a gap year (if our kids can do it then why not us?) and we enjoyed our first ski season so much that it has become a way of life. We love the snow, the mountains and skiing with passion; chalet hosting enables us to live the dream. We have numerous testimonials from past guests and students and feel well qualified to show others how to do it.

Coco Cookery, our cookery school for chalet hosts, offers a very personal service and we open our home to our students. Many have become friends and when we hear afterwards they've landed a job, well... it's what it's all about, isn't it?

41155969R00094

Printed in Poland
by Amazon Fulfillment
Poland Sp. z o.o., Wrocław